# FUEL
## The
# FIRE

5/99

Randy

my very Best to you

with Fond Aloha

Brad

*"Brad's thirst for an understanding of great performance with serenity has never diminished. I have listened as he mesmerized audiences with his powerful lectures. I have hoped he would reduce his spirit and wisdom to written form."*

— Bill Curry, Football Analyst for ESPN and Director of National Consortium for Academics and Sports

*"Exciting, stimulating and helpful. Brad Yates' passion for people and for the field of performance psychology comes through in every energized sentence of this book. This man has spent his lifetime helping people realize their potential."*

— René Tillich, Ph.D., Clinical Psychologist

*"Brad has a way of breaking down complex issues into amazingly simple and straightforward objectives. The concept of HiLevel shows you how to focus and see things that are likely hidden in the back of your mind. It brings them forward into a very clear and understandable light. The ability to achieve – focused, confident, and satisfied with one's self – has never been easier."*

— Robby Naish, World Champion Windsurfer and Businessman

*"Whether windsurfing, canoe paddling or maintaining my focus through medical school or residency, I have found the HiLevel process incredibly valuable. Brad's enthusiasm and commitment to fitness and balance in life are sure to inspire."*

— Dr. Bruce Eliashof, Psychiatrist
and HiLevel Team Rider

*"Finally, a 'training manual' for us Water People with a mind AND a heart. On any page you'll lock into a powerful reminder for your brain. Every aspiring pro should be handed a copy WITH their rules book. And EVERY rated pro should keep it in hers/his duffel for just those moments when. . . ."*

— Bernie Baker,
*SURFER MAGAZINE*

*"Many of the processes I found effective in athletic competition are well represented in this book. The practical, healthy approach to personal achievement is interesting and refreshing, especially its emphasis on participation and valuing the process more than a first place finish."*

— Matt Biondi, Winner of
11 Olympic Medals

*"To express the complexity of so many variables in livable terms is to approach a perfection that few people can obtain. Brad's fantastic work has been refined over time and daily practice. His success is measured by the people you read about here. They have taken these very straightforward ideas and use them in their pursuit of excellence. It is an outstanding way to approach performance—be it sports, work, or simply life."*

— Maui Meyer,
Entrepreneur

*"Brad's love for people and burning desire to help them become the best they can be has motivated this most inspirational book. Share it with everyone!"*

— Larry New, Georgia Tech Director-Homer Rice Center for Sports Performance and Total Person Program

*"I'm Stoked! Fuel the Fire is a great book. Brad has captured the essence of what it means to be Committed."*

— Kenny Bradshaw, the Star of the Biggest "Big Wednesday"

# Perform With Passion

## Brad Yates

▲ ▲ ▲ ▲ ▲

**HiLevel Productions**

Honolulu, Hawaii

## HiLevel Productions
Box 61866
Honolulu, Hawaii  96839

© Copyright 1998, G. Bradford Yates
ISBN 0-682-23878
Library of Congress Catalog Card Number: 98-96769

**Photo Credits**

**Front Cover**

Waimea Bay Shorebreak
North Shore, Oahu
Darrell Wong

**Back Cover**

**Surfer**
Kenny Bradshaw
Sunset Beach
North Shore, Oahu
Late evening, late takeoff
Shot by Bernie Baker from
the water.

**Runner**
Brad Yates
Punahou School
Honolulu, Hawaii
Steve Wilkings

**Kayaker**
Maui Meyer
Husum Falls, Washington
Class 5 drop
Shot by Jan Meyer

**Mountain Biker**
Jack Lutey
Sunset Hills
North Shore, Oahu
Bernie Baker

**Windsurfer**
Robby Naish
Diamond Head, Maui
Darrell Wong

*To all of you who shared your fire with me.*

*You have arrived,*

*you have fulfilled your dream,*

*you have learned to express your fire.*

— Brad Yates

# Foreword

It was my friend Brad Yates, who introduced me to the field of performance psychology, a contrast to my own area of competence – clinical psychology with its emphasis on psychopathology. Performance psychology emphasizes growth and the achievement of what Brad refers to as HiLevel performance. His ability to help people maximize their potential and his enjoyment in this lifetime work have greatly impressed and interested me.

I think Brad's particular approach is exciting, stimulating and helpful. Every sentence in his book is energized as he incorporates familiar psychology concepts into the context of performance. He presents a cogent argument for the beneficial effects of self-awareness and, conversely, shows how defensiveness and self-deception lead to performance blocks. The parallels here between issues of personality development and performance enhancement are striking.

My own experience with this book shows that it is to be lived, rather than read from cover to cover and shelved. Each section focuses on particular issues, which are most compelling when addressed in actual struggle. I think the best way to maximize the usefulness of *Fuel the Fire* is to read it once so that one knows what is offered and where to find each part. Then, as a specific problem comes up in one's performance, find the appropriate section and read it over a number of times.

I also recommend reading the book aloud to oneself. I have had the exclusive privilege and pleasure of hearing Brad read sections to me in his deep voice, expressing all the passion he has for the subject. Maybe he will also make *Fuel the Fire* into an audio book for all of us to enjoy.

— René Tillich, Ph.D.

# Prologue

I teach my passion—sports psychology—and have followed this creed all my life: *do what you love and love what you do.* Another expression from the East—*teach what you need to learn*—aptly describes the process I went through in learning to teach my passion.

I have for years been driven to understand and teach the process of "giving it your best," a process I like to refer to as "HiLevel Performance." Excellence and "HiLevel" are synonymous in this sense. And the lessons or steps that make up the HiLevel process are a reflection of the careful analysis and learning I have undergone as an athlete, teacher, parent, coach, writer, and counselor.

As an athlete, I learned to value hard work. At Georgia Tech, I was known as an over-achiever, an identity I hated at the time, but now appreciate. I played because I outworked the guys ahead of me. I learned to pay the price, to be hard-nosed and mentally tough. Coaches, using an expression common in the South, said of me, "That dog will hunt!"

As a surfer, I faced the challenge and fear of steep takeoffs. I invented my own system for mental training. I learned how to run with my feelings, to think about the take-off at Sunset—where the world's best big wave hits the North Shore of Oahu—and feel the edge control; the contact my feet made with the board as I drove my weight forward and down a wave; the speed of the board and power of the turn as the force of the fin, tail, and rail drove me forward. Over and over I imagined this scene and felt myself make the wave. Gradually, confidence in my ability was planted as I learned to listen to my body.

I also learned to accept my limits. As a windsurfer and snowboarder, I am as active and competitive as possible. When my body doesn't agree with the standards I set, I know the value of "downtime management."

As a teacher, I recognize when I am attached, that is, bound to a feeling that my position is right. Such a feeling can prevent one from being open to feedback, new ideas, or opinions. I have learned, however, that when I operate from this position I am very ineffective. I know now how to accept feedback or messages from my body: feelings and sensations generated by actions. I also know how to listen to messages from others regarding my performance.

As a parent, I have learned to relax, focus, and let go. At the age of seven, my son Reyn scored a goal in a soccer game and I got a red card

# Key Ingredients

## Interest

Interest is powerful. It keeps you present.

Throughout my education, I was determined to prove that I was not a student. I was a jock. I won again and again. My grades represented the efforts of someone who was not interested in academics. At the age of thirty-three, I had a wife and young son. I was teaching full-time. I decided to go back to school. I lived forty-five miles away from my job and the university. For the first time, I became "interested" and began making straight A's. I finally understood what it was like to be a student: starting the assignments when they were given, writing about my true interests. I asked questions in class. I had conferences with my teachers. At last, I experienced fire in the classroom.

## Intensity

Intensity carries you through. It bolsters momentum and confidence.

Cathy is the art director in charge of making TV commercials for a large and powerful company. She was headed to New York to shoot an important commercial. She was anxious. Her assignment included working with a "head strong" director. She was afraid that she and her vision for the commercial would get shut down. Cathy listened to the PrimeTime tape during her flight to New York and heard the phrase: "Yes, you can. . . relax and give your best effort." She relaxed and focused on directing the commercial. She tapped into her intense desire to effectively communicate her vision. As a result, she directed an excellent commercial. She had a great time and saw the commercial have a long run.

as I celebrated his efforts. What I thought was excitement was really anxiety. I learned how to relax and breathe through these feelings I experienced. Ten years later, my son hit two free throws to win a championship game against Maryknoll in the state basketball tournament, and people commented on my relaxed manner. I was, in fact, in a meditative trance. I had learned to focus. I had learned to let go as my son

## Excitement

Excitement is powerful. It allows you to get up and stay up emotionally and physically.

Katherine was fifteen years old, a student in a summer school class. She was a dancer and her fire had gone out. Katherine was trying out for a part she had failed to land three previous times.

"So why are you doing it?" I asked her.

"Doing what?" she said to me.

I clarified, "Trying out for a part you know you can't get."

She responded, "My mother wants me to."

"So, let your mother try out!" I said.

"No," she explained, "I love to dance and I want the part."

"Good!" I told her. "Let that be your focus."

Katherine began to focus on how much she loved dancing this part. Her story ended happily: she got her fire back and the part.

## Passion

Passion wells up from commitment and love.

My friend Jon Schneller of New York is a son in a five-generation family of furniture craftsmen. In the summer of 1967 Jon and I spent endless hours surfing Ala Moana in Hawaii, the spot known by surfers around the world as "Bowls." Jon faced a big decision: return to New York to take up the family trade and carry on its business, or stay in Hawaii and surf his brain away. Jon chose to return to New York, but to deal with his sorrow of missing the surf, he dreamed of building a trimaran. He got the plans and before anyone had realized it he was building the boat. Soon he had built the boat entirely by himself, a statement to the power of commitment and love. He focused his passion and the result was a wonderful creation.

worked with me to see that he was in charge of his own life.

As a coach, I have learned what it means to "take care of business" and to "tighten the circle." Working with fine youth coaches such as Peter Balding and Scott Rigg, I have experienced the essence of what it means to make a decision and follow through with appropriate choices. Working with coach Dan Morrison, I have experienced what it means to pull people in and to build family.

As a counseling psychologist, I have learned the value of personal issues. Perfection, which can be experienced while working towards achieving excellence, always involves personal issues, which must be seen as opportunities. There are difficult personal lessons to be learned along the road to becoming the athlete and/or person you want to be. Primary personal challenges include poise, motivation, acceptance, completion, and respect. As you work through each challenge, you must choose the options that present the right lessons and avoid the options that represent resistance.

Coaches like to use the word "heart" to describe playing with determination, courage, and intensity. I like the word fire. It is simple and best reflects the interest, intensity, excitement, and passion associated with doing one's best. To understand this and teach it has been my dream. If you learn to fuel your fire and stay committed to your mission, you will feel good about yourself and your effort. Your destiny will be excellence, and you may become a standard reference in your sport.

Robby Naish, the windsurfer who defines what it means to be a professional in his sport, has won twenty-two world titles and is currently ranked number one in the waves division of the World Cup. The pro surfer Brock Little blazed his own trail and became known for his ability on the big waves. Mike Stock, a member of the USA Canoe and Kayak Team, is the youngest member of the USA Team. He gave up his senior year at Punahou School in Honolulu to train at the Olympic development center on the mainland. Erin Berg, starting setter for the University of North Carolina Volleyball Team, worked nonstop to develop her skills. They recently paid off, too, when she was named to the All Tournament Team for the 1997 Wahine Classic. Debbie Lambert, outside hitter for Stanford's Volleyball Team, worked very hard to overcome a serious knee injury and became a member of the 1996 and 1997 National Championship Volleyball Teams.

Or, your destiny may be to fall short of your expectations and, like so many of us, face learning to get on with your life. The bottom line is to feel good about yourself and apply the lessons that you have learned in all areas of your life. The simple truth is that we are people first and athletes second.

The gift that athletics offers is wrapped in hard work, and the hard work can give you back a new sense of yourself. The excellence you experience in your life will depend on your ability to work hard, resolve your issues, apply the lessons, and express your fire. You must learn to express love for yourself, love for what you are doing, and love for the important people in your life.

As you read my book please notice the following three things:

**1)** I employ examples of people who make it. In truth, you learn a lot from not making it, from experiencing failure and from going through disasters. And yes, you can learn a lot about HiLevel performance from studying other people's "suck" and how they deal with it. I have chosen to write about the "swell", that is, the positive, uplifting experiences and the people who create them.

**2)** This is a serious book because it is needed. I have spent my entire life focused on performance, studying and contemplating the people around me who performed well. To perform with excellence one needs a very serious environment. I have spent twelve years from start to finish organizing and writing this book.

**3)** Water people are the primary characters in this book: ocean athletes who have figured out how to spend their lives focused on what they love to do. While these are the athletes with whom I am most familiar, their experiences and knowledge can be understood by a Wall Street stockbroker who races bikes on Long Island, by a San Francisco dancer, a North Carolina linen manufacturer who crews in a transoceanic sailboat race, or even a New York furniture builder who decides to build an elite fiberglass boat.

The process of learning to *Fuel the Fire* is simple. Find something that interests you, get excited, generate an intense desire and learn how to express your passion for what you love to do. This book and the classic "Steps" I outline are my way of structuring the essence of performance in a manner that is clear, sequential, logical and easily understood. Use *Fuel the Fire* as a:

Jump Start – a surge of inspiration to get you going and keep you going.

Boulet Line – a source of support if what you want to accomplish resembles a radical climb.

Playbook – a series of reminders about what you already know but may have forgotten.

Survival Kit – important tools for dealing with the emotional and physical pain that can be a part of pushing your limits.

Whatever this book turns out to be for you, I trust that it will add to your pleasure of doing what you love to do.

# THE FIRE

**P**erformance excellence is like fire. You light it, fuel it, then bask in its white glow as it begins to take off on its own. The principles outlined here are tinder that will help you set yourself afire for excellence, help you maintain your bearings, and prevent you from floundering in confusion, distraction, anger, or victimhood. They will help you shine your brightest in athletic performance. There you will live your most exhilarating moments.

Excellence inspires feelings of love, passion, excitement, challenge, endorphin rushes, deep satisfaction, and winning. While I have struggled for excellence as an athlete, teacher, husband, father, speaker, and writer, I have never achieved anything without love and passion. And without something to help generate excitement – wind and surf or the lecture spotlight – there is inevitably mediocre performance.

The key to achieving excellence lies in your ability to want to work hard, and, at the same time, to live what you are doing or visualize and feel the value of your efforts. Kahea Hart summed up the role that loving to surf played in his development as a professional surfer:

> *"Follow your heart. If you want to make your living surfing, you have got to love to surf more than anything else. Nothing can even come close to surfing. Your desire to surf has got to dominate your life. To make it as a professional surfer you have to be willing to surf hard, to train hard and to surf hard some more. To learn how to make critical take-offs and surf big*

*waves with style, you have to express the*
*feelings you have for the ocean, your life*
*and yourself. Follow your heart. If you are*
*willing to work hard and you really love to*
*surf big waves, I'll see you in the line-up*
*at Sunset Beach."*

Challenge is always present for those who thrive on excellence. It never fades as the number of experiences increase. Every big wave is different. Every loop has its own symmetry that must be discovered. Professional surfer Robby Naish, who also has a strong interest in driving race cars, once said of racing: "The more I drive the more I realize that it's not the car's limits but rather my limits that represent the challenge and the risk."

Mihaly Csikszentmihalyi, author of *Flow*, demonstrated that people are the happiest when they are involved in an activity that challenges them. In his study, which has been replicated around the world, people were paged at random throughout the day. At the moment they were paged, the subjects were to fill out a questionnaire that asked several key questions about what they were doing and how it made them feel. Invariably, people were not happiest when they were watching TV, on vacation, or even involved in leisure time activities. People were the happiest when they were involved in an activity that challenged them; required full use of their skills; forced them to focus; or gave them a way to measure their success.

The physical sensations of performance excellence vary with the chosen activity. There's a deep relaxation in stretching, an "acceleration high" in wind surfing, and an almost nirvana-like state of mental activity for distance runners and swimmers. Pro surfer Kenny Bradshaw said to me one day,

*"I love the feeling that goes with being able*
*to maintain my present level of accom-*
*plishment; I guess you could say it's pride:*
*to paddle this hard, to push this hard into*
*my turns and cutbacks, to ride this length*
*of a ride while maintaining the speed and*
*position on the wave, to get into the*

*rhythm of the waves, to catch the first or*
*biggest wave in each set and to bring*
*myself so present that everything else*
*around me washes away."*

Apart from physical sensations, many other satisfactions are derived from doing an activity well. Perhaps one needs to meet a self-imposed standard of performance such as being able to get waves on a crowded day, snowboard down a double black diamond slope, or duplicate someone else's valued accomplishment. Andre Agassi once said of satisfaction,

*"I used to play tennis because I was good at*
*it. During those times I was obsessed with*
*being considered the best player in the*
*world. I got lost in my obsession with*
*winning and for a time I hated tennis.*
*Now I love tennis and I play for the right*
*reasons. I love what goes on inside of*
*those lines. I love the feeling of playing at*
*my best and I love the excitement of*
*playing for match point in the biggest and*
*most important match of the year."*

Excellence is the feeling of wanting to be the best that you can be. The feelings related to wanting to be your best come in many varieties. These feelings range from wanting to give your best effort to wanting to win or be judged the best at a particular activity. They are what motivate you to come back for more, to work hard to experience them repeatedly. Now. . . you can hope that each time you participate in your favorite activity you will experience them again. However, without a plan, you may wind up sore, tired and frustrated. *Fuel the Fire* will help you establish a HiLevel plan that will allow you to experience the feelings you associate with excellence on a regular basis.

Says Bruce Eliashof, M.D., who has followed such a plan,

*"Ever since I was a little kid, I have wanted to*
*be one of the best at whatever I do. There is a*
*feeling of excitement, a sense of mastery that*

*comes when I am totally focused and my drive to excel is closely linked to that feeling. In windsurfing, I always push myself to jump higher and sail faster. In mountain biking, it's pushing myself to get through a particularly steep section or to win a friendly race that gives me that same feeling of satisfaction. Similarly in paddleboarding, there is an excitement and intense rush that comes from paddling my hardest for an entire race; knowing that I have given my best effort—it feels so good! It's that feeling of being able to put in my best performance and experience that sense of mastery, that incredible sense of personal satisfaction. . . that is what I love the most about competition."*

Now to achieve for yourself the highest level of performance excellence you must progress through a gauntlet of personal steps. There is no other way! Every great amateur or professional athlete has done it. The steps are simple. Based on the experiences of athletes from around the world and from many generations, the Eight Steps are:

1 Know what you want and choose it.
2 Create the time to enact it.
3 Ignite your fires of mental, physical, and spiritual energy.
4 Build momentum by refining your skills.
5 Focus your awareness and commitment.
6 Build trust in yourself and performance level.
7 Work what you've learned.
8 Enjoy performance with gratitude and excitement.

In ramping up to the challenge of the eight steps, however, you must be able to focus: concentrate all of your energy on seeing your object, making your decision, performing tasks, or maintaining a feeling. Consider the point guard in basketball as he brings the ball down the court. He observes the position of everyone on the floor; he examines his options; he selects the proper play and then executes the play by combining his movement with a specific feeling. His focus throughout this process moves from external observation—the big picture action of everyone on the court—to internal focus on choosing an option. His focus shifts back and forth as he executes the play. This entire process can take place in hundredths of a second.

To focus in basketball you must be able to concentrate on what's going on outside of you and inside of you in terms of thoughts and feelings and very specific skills. To focus at this level is to stay consciously present, to be alert and yet relaxed, to isolate and hold on to appropriate thoughts and feelings, yet maintain an image of yourself performing at your very best. The challenge to focus relates to your definition of personal excellence and the feelings that are most important to you.

To enjoy the challenge of your sport, you need to be able to relax and feel confident about your skills in the face of risk. I admire the way Kenny Bradshaw, a professional surfer best known for his "guts up approach" to surfing the biggest waves possible, can relax when surfing big waves and focus on the feelings necessary to make a surfboard go faster. Says Kenny,

> *"Your legs are tight, your chest is tight, your stomach muscles are tight, your arms are tight and you are driving and pushing for all you are worth. Just about the time you are aware of these sensations you realize that you have a long way to go. Then as you level off as you trim you realize that you need to go faster. You start to feel that your board is slow, your board just doesn't feel fast enough! You stay higher in the pocket as you search for speed."*

Bradshaw has conditioned himself to focus at a level where he can accept the challenge of surfing waves that are bigger than big, to transcend his fear, to stay consciously present and give his best effort. His external focus is on the surf and on what he has to do to make the wave.

His internal focus is on selecting the right wave and on maintaining his edge control to maximize speed.

When the conditioning is there it is easier to face the risks. I can remember a time when I was totally clear what risks I was willing to accept. When Bernie Baker, *Surfer* magazine senior editor, Ed Discoli, president of Xcel Wetsuits, and I learned how to windsurf back in the summer of 1981, we all started from scratch. So being two miles off shore at Sunset Beach and not knowing how to turn around was probably—in retrospect—not a wise move. But I was willing to learn from my mistakes and accept the risks involved. I was a strong swimmer, experienced surfer, and conditioned athlete in the company of a group of close friends who had similar abilities. The risks I took to learn how to windsurf pushed the limits of safety, but I had confidence in my preparation, experience and ability in the water. For me the challenge of learning to windsurf was pure fun and worth the risks.

I can remember a time when I was totally clear that I was not willing to learn and to accept the risk. Filipe Hoffman, president of Hoffman Fabrics in Los Angeles, is a world famous waterman known for his ability to handle huge waves in a boat or on a jetski or surfboard. When he and Jeff Johnson, also a world class waterman and North Shore resident, asked me the next winter to go out in Jeff's boat to surf the outer reef, a spot called Wailua River Mouth, I was clear: I wanted no part of it. There was not one thing that appealed to me about being out in a boat or surfing waves that big. My ego was secure and the decision was a snap for me. The risk involved went way beyond the limits of what I considered safe for me and I did not have confidence in my preparation, experience or ability in waves this big. For Filipe and Jeff, the challenge to surf Wailua River Mouth was pure fun for them and worth the risks.

Focus must include the pleasurable feelings associated with your sport as well as the required skills. If your sense of pleasure overshadows your ability to execute with the required skills—for example, adjust or respond to a sudden change in your surroundings—you could end up in a dangerous situation: a runner gets into his running and ignores the danger of traffic or a weightlifter gets so focused on his sense of being strong that he attempts an unsafe lift. The positive feelings related to your activity must be balanced with an awareness of what is good for you. As the saying goes, too much of a good thing can cause trouble. Using Kenny Bradshaw's example, while he loves the speed of surfing waves this big, he continues to focus on what he has to do to make the wave.

When you enjoy the feelings from doing an activity well, you learn to focus on giving your best effort. The focus needs to switch back and forth between what you love about doing these skills and what it takes to perform these skills. Should your focus switch to the result of your efforts, that is, winning and/or dominating your opponent, then you can lose your focus and your ability to perform at this level. As Pete Sampras points out, "My most difficult match is when I win a series of points easily—too easily—and I lose my concentration. I forget what I am doing momentarily with a brain fade and then I lose my edge. I pay for it with the next several points." To maintain your edge or your focus, you need to focus on the feelings related to doing the necessary skills well. Using Bradshaw's example, while he loves feeling that he has mastered the wave, he continues to focus on the respect that he has for waves this big.

If you enjoy the feelings of being the best, then you need to focus on the skills that got you there. Presumably, they were coupled with your best effort. If your focus shifts to beating your opponent or being the best, your performance will suffer. Such thoughts are a distraction. Perhaps no other sport offers itself as a better example of the need to focus on your own skills than downhill skiing. With such a slim margin of error between balance and rhythm, every ounce of your focus needs to be on the task at hand, namely edge control.

Holly Flanders, former U.S. Olympic skier and three-time World Cup winner states, "Most great competitors know that injuries are brought on when you let yourself become unfocused." While Kenny Bradshaw loves the feeling that he is the best at riding giant waves, he continues to focus on surfing at the best of his ability.

In short, to experience those special feelings related to your sport, you must have the necessary skills, be fit, and be able to focus and relax. Your skills need to be over-learned to the point where they become automatic. In this way your focus is on your performance, not on what you need to do, could have done, or should have done. You need to have the physical and emotional fitness to maintain the intensity and direction of your focus. In this way your fitness will allow you to be in control of your action. You also must be able to relax: to concentrate all of your energy on the task at hand, to create positive thoughts and feelings about what you are doing and to eliminate all negative thoughts and feelings related to fear, anger and anxiety. The ability to relax under pressure is a function of your confidence.

Focus is always multi-faceted. You must maintain proper internal focus, rehearse your options and select courses of action. Physically and emotionally you must focus on the feeling related to proper execution of an action. The ability to have proper internal focus, to get up and stay up physically and emotionally, is a function of your fitness. Externally, while seeing the big picture, aware of everything going on around you, you must also be able to narrow your vision.

As Steven Ungerleider points out in his book, *Mental Training for Peak Performance*,

> *"Palmer, Nicklaus and others suggest moving from one intensely focused arena to a valley of relaxation as needed; that is, experience your golf game as a two-tiered state of being—first learn how to focus intensely and second, learn how and when to let down and move into a complete state of relaxation."*

The ability to change states from intensity to relaxation is a good example of the need to be able to shift focus.

At the same time, you must stay consciously present. Be aware of what has just happened and be ready to make necessary corrections. Be able to let go, that is, process and release any and all emotions related to not doing well. Let go of negative thoughts and feelings associated with your performance. There are often moments of not performing well, something which is sometimes referred to as "tanking." This is nothing less than hanging onto the negative thoughts and feelings related to your performance.

To experience moments of performance excellence you need to realize the truth of the following statement from Mikaly Csikszentmihalyi, "Enjoyment does not depend on what you do, but on how you do it." The key to how you do it is in focus.

Ideally, the role that psychology plays in sports is to teach you how to make full use of your skills to give your best effort under pressure. Giving your best effort under pressure involves learning how to coordinate and maintain your mental, physical, and spiritual energies. When you can coordinate or focus all of the energy that is available to you, you are making full use of your skills.

Mentally, you are able to give your best effort when you have confidence in your ability, when you can overcome your fear and anger, and when you can relax under pressure. Physically, you are able to give your best effort when you have the physical strength and conditioning and the emotional energy to focus, to stay present. Spiritually, you are able to give your best effort when you have the faith in your ability to follow through with your commitment. When you put all three together, the mental toughness, the ability to focus, and the faith in yourself, what you have is your own fire.

Deepak Chopra, author of *The Seven Spiritual Laws of Success*, defines success as "the continued expansion of happiness and the progressive realization of worthy goals. Success is the ability to fulfill your desires with effortless ease." The "expansion of happiness," "the progressive realization," and the "effortless ease" that Chopra refers to are the result of an attitude that can take you beyond just a willingness to move forward, one that is eager for hard work.

The creation of personal excellence will require everything you have to give and in the process it will give you back a new sense of yourself. The Eight Steps offer you an opportunity to establish your direction, be clear of your intentions, and express all of your passion as you learn to work hard and experience all of the joy that goes with doing what you love.

The HiLevel Process allows you to set your goal, then provides you with a plan for achievement. You must get beyond the "thou shalt"; this is not about what you think you are supposed to do. As Joseph Campbell said, "You must slay the 'thou shalt' dragon."

PrimeTime is about doing what you truly want to do. It is working through the Eight Steps, from deciding what you want (defining PrimeTime), to achievement (the creation of PrimeTime). The steps represent a blueprint for giving your best effort, a control panel that gives you feedback about how you are doing, and a set of directions for getting from point A to point B.

In creating PrimeTime—experiencing those special moments associated with doing the activity you love to do—you learn how to 1) refine and organize your energy, 2) express the feelings that will guide you, and 3) enter a cycle of learning and growing.

You must be clear about what you want to achieve; to show up rested and ready to perform—mentally, physically and spiritually—and be prepared to keep working toward your goal. As you focus on specific skills, you must know your feelings, relax and be confident that you will perform up to your standards, be able to handle upsets, and support yourself and teammates.

# Talking Fire

Throughout this book I use terms that express my feelings for the process of learning to give one's best effort.

## Fire
Fire expresses the heart and soul of excellence. . . the interest, intensity, excitement, and passion you have for what you love to do.

## PrimeTime
Special moments when you feel the fire: feelings associated with
Preparation. . . anticipating the challenge in front of you.
Performance. . . executing up to your standards and beyond.
Reflection. . . contemplating what you have just accomplished.

## HiLevel
The mental toughness, focus and follow through that represents the strength of will and faith in yourself. A HiLevel person manifests these qualities.

## HiLevel Performance
The ability to give your best effort, to express your fire.

## The HiLevel Process
The Eight Steps that provide the skills needed to fuel your fire and achieve excellence.

The presence of fear may prevent you from expressing your feelings or love for your activity. I remember working with a diver named Brad, who won the state championships in springboard diving in his junior year. During his senior year, he hit his head on the end of the diving board during a routine dive. The fear of repeating the accident became a major obstacle for him: his diving suffered and his school work suffered. In fact, every area of his life was so affected by this fear that he was "stuck in his tracks."

To combat his fear, Brad broke his responsibilities down into day-, hour-, even minute-sized portions. He learned to stay consciously present by focusing on the feelings of a specific required skill. Mentally, he relaxed, yet concentrated to regain his confidence. He used affirmations and positive self-talk to work his basic diving and study skills. In the state championship meet, he put it all together and was able to express his feelings and passion for diving.

You will enter the cycle of learning and growing when you can be clear with yourself about why you want to do it, can adapt to change, can take care of yourself, can accept yourself and situations beyond your control, and can become all you can be yet still want more. The ability to create PrimeTime puts you into a zone of tweaking that demands that you learn from lessons of experience and incorporate adjustments into your performance and personal growth.

*Robby Naish is clear about what he wants to do.* He has built his life around his desire to be a professional windsurfer. During this time he continued to find a way to be successful in competition, to handle the rigors of travel, to promote the sport, and simply make his living doing what he loves to do.

*Robby adapted to change* by keeping up with advancements in equipment. He even helped design the present day equipment which is both super-light and super-responsive. He learned and maintained the skills he needed to handle this equipment, accepting the challenge of change yet becoming creative with it. When Robby sails out at Diamond Head after a long absence, it is readily apparent that he is still the hottest guy in the water. He lists his proudest moment as, "when people say I'm sailing now better than ever."

*Robby learned to take care of himself.* For a number of years Robby suffered from a serious back injury:

> *"When my back started causing me problems, I was severely limited in what I could do. I was unable to run, stretch in certain ways, or surf for long because of the strain it put on my back. I maintained my fitness with pushups, krunches, toe-raises,*

*leg lifts, and knee bends, and I occasion-*
*ally lifted weights. I became very careful to*
*match my time in the water with equal*
*amounts of rest. I learned during this time*
*to be super-sensitive to feedback from my*
*body."*

Robby's injury and its limitations on his performance are now a thing of the past, further proof of his ability to learn and grow.

*Robby learned to accept time out of the water.* He grew up being able to sail whenever he wanted to. With increased responsibilities, he learned to accept the reality of time limits:

*"I just spent three weeks in Europe on*
*business and I didn't touch a windsurfer.*
*It's tough! It is very difficult for me to be*
*out of the water, but at the same time it*
*keeps me motivated mentally to want to*
*sail when my schedule is right. There are*
*lots of times when I am unable to sail for*
*two and three weeks at a time. I have*
*learned to deal with the negative effects of*
*downtime."*

Robby talks about becoming:

> *"My biggest asset is my self-motivation and drive. I have never had a trainer or a coach to tell me what to do or to help motivate me. I am self-driven. I have been able to coach myself. I have been out there sailing hard because I love it. For twenty years, I have been driven by the excitement of this sport and my love for doing it. Windsurfing has never seemed like work, nor have I ever had to push myself to sail or perform."*

*Robby wants more:* "The sport is still changing and I want to compete on as high a level as I can. I would love to win a world title again. Right now I'm in second place overall, and I would like to do better."

In summary, the steps to HiLevel involve hard work, discipline and the eagerness to learn. The hard work will allow you to experience PrimeTime, the discipline will carry over into every area of your life, and the lessons will provide you with a source of continued growth.

Light your fire of personal excellence. Fuel the fire eagerly. Enjoy the fire.

The HiLevel process begins when you decide what you want to achieve. To decide what you want to achieve is a function of your ability to be proactive and to establish your own reality. To be proactive is to decide to take control of your life. When it comes to decisions of this magnitude there are two extremes. Draw a straight line across a sheet of paper. Put "Extreme #1" all the way to the left and "Extreme #2" all the way to the right. Write Conformity under #1 and Rejection under #2.

# STEP ONE

# Know what you want and choose it.

**Extreme #1  Extreme #2**
**Conformity    Rejection**

Extreme position #1 involves a position of total conformity. In this position you make one decision, namely to follow a set of rules, a specific plan or strategy. You work hard to be the best, to gain approval, to achieve your goal. In making the decision to conform, your focus takes you outside of your feelings. This decision to conform is a potential trap that involves "doing it right" as opposed to "doing it with feelings." Without questioning authority, yourself or others, you can easily lose sight of your feelings related to your ability to give your best effort.

Extreme #2 is the position of total rejection. In this position, you make one decision, namely not to play. You reject the rules and the game. In making one decision—to rebel, to go against the grain—your focus takes you outside of your feelings. The decision to reject is also a potential trap that involves "not doing" as opposed to "doing." Without questioning yourself and your motives, you can easily lose an awareness of the feelings related to what you really want to do.

Avoid the extremes. Operating in extreme positions #1 or #2 is to be attached. Attached is the act of being bound to a belief or a decision.

The bad news about being attached is that when you are bound to a belief or a decision, you are stuck: you are limited in your vision. Your focus takes you outside of yourself and you are acting outside of your feelings. Without questioning yourself and your motives, you can easily lose sight of what you really want.

The good news is that the fact that you are attached is an indication of how much you care, how important your performance is to you. When you care this much you can learn to question yourself and to be clear in your motives.

To be proactive is to learn how to make decisions based on your principles. Sam Keen, author of the book, *Hymns to An Unknown God*, said, "The most important decision we have to make is the decision that we can make decisions." Keen is suggesting that we actively participate in learning how to make decisions. Learning how to make decisions is to question authority—in a respectful and loving way: question coaches, friends, and most of all question yourself and then decide to play, each day, moment to moment. Decide to play at a level that feels right to you. In this way, your feelings are an indication of your principles. To learn how to be proactive, practice making decisions based on your feelings.

Which is hard work! To make a decision based on your feelings requires the discipline to step back and evaluate your feelings in an objective manner. Being objective, when it comes to your feelings, can result in some difficult decisions.

Matt Biondi, the winner of eleven Olympic medals, recently had a difficult decision to make. Matt was offered two hundred thousand dollars to attempt a comeback for the '96 Olympics. The money was put up by some promoters that wanted to capitalize on the publicity of his comeback. The money was guaranteed, and the only stipulation was that he be serious about his training. He did not have to make the team, or even do well.

In making his decision, Matt made the right decision for the right reasons. His decision was not for either extreme; he made his decision based on his feelings of what was right for him and his wife Kirsten. He and Kirsten took two weeks to make the decision. They meditated, prayed, and talked about it, then repeated the process. At the end of two weeks, Matt graciously said, "No, thank you; my heart isn't into it." In saying no to the money, he was being proactive; not because swimming for a company, for money, for a sponsor, or for the Olympics is inherently wrong, but swimming for these reasons was wrong for Matt. At this particular time it did not feel right for him.

Matt could have operated at extreme position #1. He could have accepted the money; after all, two hundred thousand dollars is a lot of money for an Olympic swimmer, even if he has won eleven medals. Matt could have forced himself to train hard, to go through the motions. In that case, his commitment would have been to his sponsors, the money, the Olympics, but not necessarily to himself. He could have based his decision on his need for control or attention or approval. He could have based his decision on a decision that he made a long time ago, namely, that he could accept any and all challenges.

# Total Commitment

**Mentally:** believe in yourself and your ability, and that what you are doing is the right thing.
**Physically:** accept the physical and emotional discomfort that comes with learning to give your best effort.
**Spiritually:** make the choices that are consistent with what you want to have happen, and ground your performance in self-acceptance.

Conversely, he could have operated at extreme position #2. He could have made his decision based on his need to reject, to rebel. He could have given the promoters "attitude." When I asked him what it would have taken to make a comeback, he said, "The love of my sport, the will to push the limits of my ability, and the pure joy associated with doing what I love." To train as hard as an Olympic swimmer, and be able to experience love and joy, involves the freedom to decide each moment to push yourself and stay consciously present.

It is a much greater challenge to make the right decision for the right reasons. Making the right decision for the right reasons involves an awareness of your principles, what feels right for you. In Matt's case, what felt right to him was to say no to the money and focus on creating a life for himself and his new bride, Kirsten.

Decisions which "feel right" allow you to maintain your clarity of what is important to you. This clarity allows you to avoid distractions and experience the success and satisfaction related to your efforts. Such decisions give you the ability to stay present and give your best effort. The feelings related to your decision form the basis for your commitment.

Learning to be proactive is a process. It is the realization that decisions at this level involve: deciding, taking a risk, courageously confronting anxiety, accepting outcomes, and deciding again.

While being proactive requires a decision to take control of your life, the control is fleeting at best. It is really a decision to do your best and to accept the results. Doing your best, by definition, demands that you are totally committed mentally, physically, and spiritually.

Mentally, your belief will create your experience. To do your best you must believe in what you are doing. In Matt's case, accepting the money and attempting a comeback could have been the right decision for him had he believed that it was the right thing for him to do.

Physically, your feelings are what allow you to take care of the business at hand. When you are involved in pushing your emotional and physical limits, you must be free to welcome the pain, to see the discomfort as an integral part of your program. Matt, for example, no longer had the passion for swimming that allowed him to push himself to reach a level of winning eleven Olympic medals.

Spiritually, your choice manifests your experience. In order to accept the outcome of your efforts you must feel good about yourself and your ability to make choices which are consistent with what you want to have happen. Feeling good about yourself and having faith in your ability to follow through is dependent on your clarity of the why behind your efforts. Again, in Matt's case, as an Olympic athlete he was clear that he loved his sport and that his will to compete at this level was based on "the pure joy associated with doing what I love." In the same way, when he turned down the money, he was clear that his Olympic swimming career was complete.

In summary, to achieve what you want, be proactive. Stay in the middle and practice making decisions all day long. Learn to base your decisions on your feelings. Establish your reality. The reality of what you can achieve can only be defined by you, determined by the depth of your commitment.

This brings us full circle, back to the questions: how hard are you willing to work and how much of a risk are you willing to take? The answers to these questions can be found in your feelings. Your feelings are central. Daniel Goleman, in his book *Emotional Intelligence*, asks you to understand the concept of emotional intelligence and to appreciate that your "EQ is more important than your IQ." When you consider that the base of all performance is emotion, and that the neurological passageways of performance are all stored in your brain as emotional memories, it is easy to see that Goleman is right. In terms of your performance, your EQ is more important than your IQ.

According to Goleman, emotional intelligence has to do with: 1) being aware of your feelings and understanding what they mean; 2) being in control of your feelings, able to express them in an appropriate manner; and 3) empathy, that is, being at one with the feelings of others.

Awareness and understanding deal with the ability to determine your desire to achieve a goal and how much of yourself you are willing to invest in defining your reality. In his book called *Flow*, Mikaly Csikszentmihalyi says,

> *"competition improves experience only as long as attention is focused primarily on the activity itself. If extrinsic goals such as beating the opponent, wanting to impress an audience, are what one is concerned about, then competition is likely to become a distraction, rather than an incentive to focus consciousness on what is happening."*

Being able to control your feelings is to control your focus, to stay present, to focus on making decisions that are consistent with what you want to have happen. One of the features of empathy is that the more you can feel for someone else the more you can feel for yourself. The more you can feel for yourself the more you can feel for others. The more you can feel for yourself the more you can make decisions that are in your best interest.

In short, to establish your own reality, develop what Goleman refers to as your emotional intelligence. Build an awareness of your own feelings, learn to express them in an appropriate way and practice having empathy for others.

As a coaching point, write down what you want to achieve and then share it out loud with someone you trust. Sharing out loud what you want to achieve will perform two important functions: clarity and affirmation. As you share out loud what you want to achieve, ask your friend to challenge you with some tough questions. If you accept the challenge and you feel strong and confident as you reply, then you are on the right track. If on the other hand, you get defensive and you feel anxious, then maybe you are attached and you need to reconsider. As you share out loud what you want to achieve with feeling, you are conditioning your subconscious mind to believe that you can do it!

As a second coaching point, beware of unrealistic expectations. Mitch Gaylord talks about the danger of having unrealistic expectations. As a member of the 1988 Olympic Gymnastic Team, Gaylord was part of the effort that brought home the first-ever gold medal in the team competition. Gaylord also won two individual medals, one gold and one silver. While his teammates celebrated and people rushed to congratulate him, Gaylord felt nothing. He was unable to forgive himself for a simple mistake that he had made in an earlier event.

While the mistake did not affect the team score or cost him a medal, he was furious with himself, and his anger quickly turned to depression. He spent the next year attempting to kill the pain with drugs. Though Gaylord can now talk openly about the absurdity of his reaction to making such a simple mistake, his story underlines the need to avoid becoming attached to a sense of perfection and allow others to assist in critiquing and understanding your performance.

A healthier and more realistic approach is to focus on what is important. Firstly, there is the love of your sport—what Biondi referred to as, "the love of my sport, the will to push the limits of my ability and the pure joy associated with doing what I love." Secondly, there are the feelings related to doing your sport well. Make sure you are having fun or seeing the value of your efforts; if not, ask yourself, "Why not?"

Betsy Somerville was clear and proactive. I first met Betsy in her tenth grade year of high school, in my required health class. On one particular day, Betsy came late to class and was so angry that she couldn't sit down. After some coercion we got her to sit down and explain her anger. Just as she would start to explain her situation, her anger would flare and she would be up again walking around in a rage. Finally, she agreed to tell us what happened without the emotion.

Betsy had gone on a school-approved trip to Japan to compete in a very important tennis tournament (which she won). When she returned to school she found out that her absence caused her to fail a very important math test. When she went to the dean, he explained that while the school had approved her trip, the teacher in question had the right to treat the absence as unexcused.

Betsy had just come from the dean and announced that she was going to leave school and find a school that would give her the freedom to travel. No one in the class, including myself, could believe that she was serious. How could she possibly leave one of the best schools in the country? To Betsy the answer was simple. She wanted a full scholarship to college to play tennis. In order to get a full scholarship she needed to be rated in the world. To be rated in the world, she needed to play in tournaments throughout the world.

We were all convinced she should stay. Betsy, however, was clear that she was leaving. Later, I was concerned enough to call Betsy's mother, who informed me that Betsy had already found a new school and that it was a done deal.

For the next two years, Betsy traveled throughout the world playing in major tennis tournaments. Her new school allowed her to miss ten weeks of school at a stretch and to complete her work through correspondence. Her plan worked. She achieved her world ranking, and she eventually accepted a full scholarship to the University of Arizona.

A few years after she had graduated from college, I asked her about her major decision and she replied,

> *"I made the right decision and I'm proud that I had the clarity to know what I needed to do for me, and for my career. I made my dream come true, playing tennis in college and then to play on the pro tour was pure PrimeTime for me. I would not have missed this time in my life for anything."*

Betsy took control of her life and in the process made a very difficult decision and based it on her principles, established her own reality, focused on the love of her sport, and had fun creating PrimeTime.

**W**here there is a will there is a way. Or, according to Nietzsche, the great philosopher of the human will, "He who knows a 'why' for living, will surmount almost every 'how'."

In Step One, we defined PrimeTime in terms of what you want to achieve. In Step Two, you need to create the time and energy to make it happen. The ability to create this time and energy starts and ends with you. Do you believe that you can create this time and energy? If the answer is yes, then your positive attitude will allow you to tap into your creativity and find a way.

Consider the case of my friend and colleague, Harry,

# STEP TWO
# Create the time to enact it.

who was strapped for time. With a young family and a full-time teaching and coaching position, he had little time for his own training. His solution was to bring in and store in his locker at school five outfits every Sunday afternoon, clothes for each day of the week. Each morning he ran to school (a distance of about three miles), showered, got dressed and went to class. At the end of each day he repeated the process and ran home. Harry believed he could create the time and energy he needed to train each day and he did.

Consider the case of every dedicated swimmer, gymnast, surfer, or triathlon athlete. They find the time and energy to train or surf for at least four hours per day. So what about you? How much time and energy do you need to train and perform up to your standards?

My purpose in presenting the following material is to give you an awareness of some basic techniques that could assist you in the process of learning to create the time and energy you need. Specifically, these techniques relate to learning how to: 1) condition yourself to believe that you can create the time and energy you need; 2) create an ongoing training schedule that allows you to refine your efforts and improve your performance; 3) listen to the signals your body is sending you and make good decisions regarding your need for rest; and 4) build and cement your level of commitment.

My purpose is not to tell you how to create the time and energy you need. The creation of the time and energy you need is determined by you, and ultimately comes down to how much you want it. In studying people like my friend Harry, who are strapped for time, I have revisited the simple truth: "Where there is a will, there is a way." The people who have the will, find a way to train hard and the ones who don't. . . complain. Having the will is a product of caring; as you read, please examine how important the creation of PrimeTime is to you.

First of all, believe that *you can* create PrimeTime. The idea that you can create the time and energy you need to train and perform up to your standards is a function of your belief system. At the core of your belief system is your self esteem, the sum of the feelings you have for yourself and your ability. Underneath these feelings are your principles, the basis of your decision making process. To create the time and energy you need, align your beliefs, feelings, and choices.

Believe in yourself mentally, maintain a positive attitude and practice making positive statements regarding your ability to create the time and energy you need. Push yourself physically to train hard and focus on the feelings that come with an increased sense of physical and emotional well-being. Maintain your commitment spiritually and acknowledge yourself for having the discipline to follow through on your decision to create the time and energy you need.

The alignment of your beliefs, feelings and choices will coordinate your mental, physical and spiritual energy. This coordination will condition your mind to believe that you can, your body to feel that you can, and your spirit to have faith that you can.

Consider what you want to achieve. Making it happen is dependent on your ability to establish and execute a plan. As Stephen Covey points out, "All things are created twice. There is the mental or first creation and a physical or second creation to all things." Your statement about what you want to achieve in Step 1 is the first creation. A plan in the form of a training schedule is preparation for the second creation.

Keep the training schedule simple. Create a training schedule that will fit your personality and the way you like to organize your time and energy. It should allow you to plan your week for optimal performance, growth and fun. In this regard, some people are "planners." They like to follow a schedule, love routine and discipline. They prefer a step, step, step. . . straight line approach. Kenny Bradshaw is a planner. He acknowledges that his ability to plan and organize his time and energy is a big part of his success today. Kenny follows a very strict schedule that impacts every area of his life, from diet, to how and when he trains, how many waves he catches an hour, even how he shapes his surfboard. If Kenny does it, it is part of his plan and you can bet he has thought about it.

Then there are "players" who just love to have fun, love spontaneous activity and open-ended schedules. They want to be free to create their own energy on their own terms. Robby Naish is a player. He acknowledges that the fun he has windsurfing is a big part of his success today. He is always ready to have fun; windsurfing, surfing, racing cars, whatever the activity, he is always ready. Robby moves from one activity to the next with a seemingly unlimited amount of energy. He thrives on a schedule that allows him the freedom to be spontaneous and creative. To the most minute detail, if Robby does it, it is because it feels right and you can bet he will express himself.

Planners like to get better and players like to have fun. Planners, in an effort to get better, may be tempted to go too fast, to increase the duration and intensity of their training ahead of their ability to handle this level of training. The result can be unnecessary soreness or injury. To planners I suggest: slow down and make sure you are having fun.

The players, with their focus on having fun, may get bored with the routine of a regular training program. I suggest to players: use your creativity to make what you've decided to do fun, even when there may seem to be a lack of spontaneity and freedom.

Pick a time on Sunday for planning your training sessions for the week. Experiment with different times of day until you find a time that works for you. Include sessions in training and competition to fit your particular needs. Planning your training sessions for the week will allow you to budget your time and keep you on track.

Each day or each week define what you want to accomplish and call it HiLevel. List your performance and outcome goals. Performance goals have to do with the part of your performance you can control, that is, your attitude, intensity, discipline, and ability to have fun. Outcome goals have to do with the part of your performance that you cannot control: the conditions, the competition, the success of the people around you, in short, everything that is outside of your attitude and your effort.

Use the scale, **Lo 1 2 3 4 5 Hi**, to evaluate your performance each day. The evaluation process will assist you in gaining an awareness of what works for you and maintain the momentum gained from your hard work. Evaluating each session is really important in activities where you are working hard to maintain or build the intensity of your training sessions, such as paddling, running, or weight training.

Record the major lessons gained from your daily evaluations. This evaluation will allow you to improve your ability to plan and perform. Recording your lessons is an opportunity to make sure you have learned from your experience and, in some cases, prevent you from repeating the same mistake.

Maintain the balance of health and fitness. Consult your evaluations often to be certain that you are following a schedule that supports your health and your fitness. Establish a place to record your resting pulse each day. Making an effort to monitor the balance of your health and fitness will keep you from getting sick, hurt or both.

Be ready at any time to HALT. As you push the limits of your ability, there will be times when you will experience negative thoughts and feelings. HALT is an acronym for the presence of negative energy, the presence of which is a warning to stop and evaluate. H = Hunger; A = Anger; L = Lonely; and T = Tired. The presence of any one of these signals is reason for concern, reason to evaluate what is going on with your program, with *you*!

The presence of Hunger is a signal to check your eating habits. Are you eating the wrong foods or not enough of the right foods? What about your fluids? Dehydration is a form of hunger. Also, check your spirit; hunger can be signal of boredom.

The presence of Anger is a signal to check in with yourself, to ask yourself the question, "What about this situation is making me angry?" Anger can be a signal that you need to communicate; perhaps you have a need to control or you have an unrealistic expectation. Anger cannot be allowed to go unresolved or unprocessed. It builds up and the build-up can be extremely toxic, to you and your relationships.

The presence of Loneliness is a signal to check in with your intentions. Namely, what is missing in your life? Loneliness can be a signal that you have lost sight of your original intention; perhaps you feel like you are missing out on some fun and/or you need to adjust your training schedule.

Being Tired is a signal to check in with your attention, that is, your ability to maintain a healthy life-style. Fatigue can be a signal that you need to get more rest, eat better, lighten up the physical and emotional load, take a break and listen to some music or just plain have more fun.

The spiritual component of your performance is essential. It has to do with your ability to be committed, to be true to yourself, to follow through, to make a decision and then to make the appropriate choices. Part of being committed is the need to acknowledge the source of your inner strength and support. Certainly family, coaches, peers, and significant others are part of this group. Perhaps you need to acknowledge God or some other form of higher power or spirituality. The suggestion here is to take the time to strengthen and enrich your spiritual program. Reflect, contemplate, meditate, pray and/or practice those behaviors that build your faith and enhance your ability to be committed, to do what is right for you.

# Create PrimeTime

*Plan* your time and energy effectively.
*Evaluate* and grow from your efforts.
*Balance* hard work, play, and health.
*Recognize* the "red flags" that signal special needs.
*Develop* a spiritual program of renewal and commitment.

As you do this and create PrimeTime you will discover how to express your fire, that special way of expressing all of your desire and passion. This fire will fuel your performance and engender courage to deal with fear and anger, two emotions which tend to linger unless they are dealt with head-on.

In terms of your health, all feelings are recorded in your body on a chemical level. Positive feelings produce a chemical reaction which produces a sense of well-being, enhance the functioning of your immune system, and increase the efficiency of your internal organs. Negative feelings which are allowed to persist produce toxins in your bloodstream. These decrease the functioning of your immune system and put a strain on internal organs.

The key word here is "persist." A tinge of anger, fear, or anxiety can be a good thing, a source of motivation. However, when anger, fear or anxiety is the driving force behind your actions, the situation can be poisoning.

Consider the "fight or flight" response, which is basically a triple whammy. Firstly, anger, fear, or pain sends a message to the most primitive level of your brain, and adrenaline is automatically released into your blood. As the adrenaline reaches your heart, it speeds up, putting your mind and body into a "hyperactive state." This hyperactivity takes away from your ability to operate in the present and puts a real strain on your entire system.

Secondly, after the adrenaline leaves the heart, it turns into cortisol, a toxic substance which has to be removed from the bloodstream. The work of this removal falls on the immune system, putting added strain on this vital system. Should you be on the verge of getting sick or recovering from an intense workout or injury, this added strain could be a serious blow to your overall health.

Thirdly, some psychologists suggest that your subconscious mind responds to your emotional distress as a request for more information. The subconscious portion of your brain begins to play a movie entitled, "All of Your Thoughts and Feelings Related to This Distress." As the movie plays, it triggers a "fight or flight" response and the cycle repeats.

Be aware of your fear and anger and make a conscious decision to take control of your situation and choose a different response. Some athletes even report that they play better in the presence of anger or fear. Greg Maddox, for example, says, "Fear helps me. Fear of not succeeding motivates me." The key point here is that Maddox uses fear as a motivator, and it quickly dissipates as he performs.

Another emotion important in the creation of PrimeTime is love, the ultimate source of your fire. As Pele said in 1977, when he retired from professional soccer, "Love is more important to our performance than anything else we can say or do. Please say with me three times—Love! Love! Love!"

Love is a feeling that originates in your soul. The soul, as Thomas Moore suggests in his book, *Care of the Soul*, "is not a thing, but a quality or a dimension of experiencing ourselves. It has to do with depth, value, relatedness, heart, and personal substance." Love is a feeling that expresses how you feel about yourself, how you feel about the people who are important to you and how you feel about what you are doing.

Love manifests itself: as a feeling of interest, the ability to stay present and focus, the energy to show that you care; as a feeling of intensity, the ability to give your best effort, the power that represents how much you care; as a feeling of excitement, the ability to "get up and stay up" physically and emotionally, the expression of your will and the strength of your character; as a feeling of passion, the ability to maintain your commitment and take care of business, the expression of the faith you have in yourself and your ability.

To experience love is to believe in love, and to believe in love is to practice being a loving and kind person. Love is an action. To express your love you need to be in contact with your soul: aware of your principles, knowing what is important to you and why; making decisions based on what feels right to you; feeling good about yourself and what you are doing; eager to work hard, to give your best effort and accept the results; and sharing, including others in your experience, tightening the circle, being thankful, showing appreciation.

> *"To experience love is to believe in love, and to believe in love is to practice being a loving and kind person. Love is an action. To express your love you need to be in contact with your soul: aware of your principles, knowing what is important to you and why; making decisions based on what feels right to you; feeling good about yourself and what you are doing; eager to work hard, to give your best effort and accept the results; and sharing, including others in your experience, tightening the circle, being thankful, showing appreciation."*

Another important part of your spiritual program is the need to renew your spirit, to nurture your soul. Renewal, in this sense, is the ability to revive the good feelings you have for yourself; be resilient, able to bounce back from tough loss; restore the good feelings you have for the people who are important to you, bond with and accept teammates, communicate and cooperate; and reestablish the good feelings you have for what you are doing, getting back into action after a lapse in concentration, a short rest, or a period of extended or forced downtime.

Ways to renew are personal. Some common means are moments of quiet reflection, writing in a journal or talking with a friend/friends you trust, reading, jogging or walking, experiencing nature, listening to music, praying, chanting, power napping, sharing an important communication and/or having a team meeting.

Essentially, the creation of the energy you need to create PrimeTime is dependent on your ability to:

**1)** **Plan**, organize your time and energy in an effective manner;

**2)** **Evaluate**, learn and grow from your efforts;

**3)** **Establish a balance**: work hard, play hard, and be healthy;

**4)** **HALT**: recognize and respond to the "red flags" that signal special needs; and

**5)** **Develop a spiritual program**, make contact with soul, find and express your love and learn how to renew the fire that enables you to maintain your commitment.

As we begin this chapter there are two quotations that I have often found highly motivating. Firstly, there is a depth of power in assumption, as Shakespeare observed: "Assume a virtue though you have it not." Secondly, lighting your own fire is an act of personal greatness which, I think, is within our reach. As John Foster has said, "One of the strongest characteristics of a genius is the power of lighting its own fire."

In Step Two, you created the time and energy to achieve PrimeTime. In step three you will learn how to light your own fire. Lighting your fire requires the confidence (the spark) to be mentally tough, the physical and emotional energy or fitness (the fire) to focus and the commitment (the fuel) to follow through.

# STEP THREE

# Ignite your fires of mental, physical, and spiritual energy.

## Confidence

Your best effort comes when you are confident and mentally tough and able to relax and perform under pressure. Mental toughness comes as you learn to incorporate four skills into every area of your life.

## Skill One

Programming your mind is the act of creating a positive environment, a positive energy in your mind, a little voice that says,

"Yes. . . I can!" The positive environment that you are working to create is in the subconscious portion of your mind. Programming your subconscious involves learning to be aware of the body's responses to certain thoughts and feelings, and using the conscious mind to generate the appropriate thoughts to produce the desired feelings in your body. The conscious mind acts on your direction. Confidence starts with you and ends with you. You are responsible for feeding the conscious mind the beliefs, the direction it needs to program the subconscious mind.

## Skill Two

Rapid and shallow breaths signal danger to the brain. Slow, steady and deep breaths signal the brain to relax. If practiced on a regular basis, deep breathing can condition the mind to relax in the face of events that would normally create anxiety. By following a strict program of deep breathing, it's possible to condition your mind and body to relax in the time it takes for one complete breath. Begin to be more sensitive to your breathing.

Practice breathing in the following fashion: take a slow, deep breath, inhaling through your nose; push your abdomen out as you breathe, allowing your rib cage to expand while you fill your lungs to their maximum capacity; pause at the top of your breath, and then slowly exhale through your mouth, forcefully contract your abdomen as you exhale, exaggerating the movement as you expel the air from your lungs; pause at the bottom of your breath, and then begin again. Learning to breathe in this manner will allow you to train your mind and body to relax.

During the course of your day take a moment to perform the following exercise. Assume a comfortable position and breathe in the manner described above. Inhale slowly, pause at the top and count the number one. Exhale slowly, pause at the bottom and count the number two. Repeat the process as you count up to the number ten. Practice seeing the numbers and focusing on your breathing. If you lose count, start the process again, beginning with number one on your next inhalation. Perform three sets of counting to ten in this manner and notice the effect that this breathing has on your ability to relax and focus.

Incorporate this breathing method into every aspect of your life. Practice taking deep breaths and pausing while you are working, training, eating, talking, or any time you need to relax and focus. There will be times when you will want to "calm down" the full action of the abdomen.

## Skill Three

Victor Frankl once said, "Relax under pressure and you'll tap into God's power." The ability to relax at will as it relates to performance, combines mental toughness and "deep muscle relaxation." Mental toughness involves commanding the mind and body to relax. The ability to relax under pressure is a spiritual matter.

"Deep muscle relaxation" releases tension from the muscle, restores circulation, aids recovery, and promotes a full range of motion. Deep muscle relaxation is best performed by alternating muscle tension with muscle relaxation. First tense the muscle in question and then relax it. During each phase, focus on the feeling in the muscle with a special emphasis on building an awareness of the feeling of relaxation compared to tension. Complete deep muscle relaxation has an emotional component. To reach this level of relaxation, command yourself to "let go" during each relaxation phase.

Note that deep muscle relaxation comes in three forms: the long version, the short version, and the recovery version. The idea is to practice the long version until the short version produces the desired result. At this point you can begin to incorporate deep muscle relaxation into the recovery phase of your performance. Experiment with the following exercises.

**The Long Version:** Sit in a comfortable position and let your body relax. Begin by curling your toes, extend your feet and hold the tension in your feet for a count of five, and then relax your feet. Moving up your body, tense your calves and hold the tension for a count of five and then relax your calves. Tense your thighs and hold the tension for a count of five, and then relax your thighs. Tense your buttocks and hold the tension for a count of five, and then relax your buttocks. Tense your abdominals and hold the tension for a count of five, and then relax your abdominals.

Now moving to your upper body, curl your fingers and make a fist and now relax your fingers. Curl your arms and hold the tension for a count of five, and then relax your arms. Tense your chest and hold the tension for a count of five, and then relax your chest. Tense your back and hold the tension for a count of five, and then relax your back. Pull your shoulders up to your ears and hold the tension for a count of five, and now relax your shoulders. Clench your teeth, squint your eyes, wrinkle your brow and hold the tension for a count of five, and now relax your mouth, face and head. For the grand finale, tense every area of your body, hold the tension for a count of five and now relaxxxxxx. . . your entire body.

**The Short Version:** Focus your attention now on your feet, calves, thighs and buttocks. Tense each of these areas and hold the tension for a count of five, and then relax your feet, calves, thighs and buttocks. Moving to your upper body, curl your fingers, make a fist, curl your arms, flex your chest and back, tighten your abdomen, pull your shoulders up to touch your ears, clench your teeth, wrinkle your forehead, squint your eyes and hold your breath and now relaxxxx. . . . Once more, and relaxxxxxxxxx. . . . Now tense your entire body, hold the tension for a count of five, . . . and relaxxxxxxxxxxxxxxx.

**The Recovery Version:** During moments of your training session, practice taking a deep breath while you tense and relax different parts of your body. In critical conditions, practice breathing as follows. You put inhaling and exhaling together with holding the breath in a constant pattern. One way to count: "one, two" (inhaling), "one, two" (holding the breath), "one, two" (exhaling), "one, two" (holding the breath), "one, two" (inhaling). After a while you get used to this pattern and don't have to count any more.

This is a powerful instrument that helps focus attention because it helps you to stop thinking, which, in turn, frees the body to do the right moves. It has been reported that relaxation is transmitted as an impulse to the nervous system, producing pleasurable feelings; to the muscles, releasing tension; and to the endocrine system, aiding in the recovery process. Relaxation during the recovery phase of your performance will be covered in "downtime management" in step five.

## Skill Four

Think in a feeling sense. Learn how to relax, then to visualize what it is you want to do. See it and feel it. The act of "seeing it and feeling it" allows the conscious mind to program the subconscious mind. The conscious mind programs the subconscious mind through the use of powerful images and feelings. The subconscious mind records these images, feelings and related actions as electrical energy. The stronger the feelings recorded by the subconscious related to the image, the more likely the actions in question will get repeated. For example, if you are surfing in challenging conditions for the first time; you will want to be able to surf with confidence. The more you visualize yourself surfing with confidence, feeling the confidence, the more likely you will be surfing with confidence.

To build confidence in yourself and your ability, practice the skills of mental training on a regular basis, at all times and under all conditions. Program your mind to provide you with the "yes. . . I can" belief in yourself. Learn to incorporate deep breathing and relaxation into all areas of your life. Learn to "think in a feeling sense," practice "seeing it" in living color, and "feeling it" with passion. Psychologists say that it takes twenty-one days to learn a new behavior or change a habit. Allow yourself this time frame and be patient with yourself.

## Fitness

The second area of importance is physical and emotional energy or fitness (the fire), which is required for focus. Maintain your base of physical and emotional fitness and practice maintaining your focus (state control). Your best effort comes when you are physically and emotionally ready, when you are able to "get up and stay up," when you are able to maintain your physical and emotional intensity and focus.

Fitness is the ability to perform physically and emotionally. It involves being ready and able to maintain the right "state" throughout your activity. The right state is the combination of a thought about what you want to do and the feeling associated with doing it. Building state control involves the development of your physical and emotional fitness, and learning how "to think in a feeling sense."

All of your physical, emotional and spiritual talent must work together in harmony. A thought about what you want to accomplish provides the picture or blueprint that sets the framework for your performance level. A feeling about what you want to accomplish activates the energy and sets your thought into action. A thought combined with a specific feeling creates a state.

Fitness calls for all of the physical, emotional, and spiritual energy you have to give. As Vince Lombardi pointed out, "Fatigue makes cowards of us all." If you run out of physical or emotional energy during the heat of your activity, you may be tempted to quit. Emotional or physical fatigue could bring you to the point of wanting to "sack the bats," that is, to give up. When fatigue sets in prior to giving your best effort, your performance level will drop and injury is likely. Consider the physical and emotional demands of your activity as you evaluate your fitness requirements.

The physical demands of your activity relate specifically to the amount of energy, strength and endurance required. The emotional demands of your activity relate specifically to state control: how much energy is required for you to relax, to focus and execute.

# Commitment

Once you have the confidence to be mentally tough you can then develop the commitment to follow through. Your best effort comes when you are committed, when you are willing to accept the responsibility for making it happen. Make a training schedule and stick to it.

The act of being committed is a learned behavior, a conditioned response to follow through on your decisions. A decision relates to a specific course of action. For example, you have decided to go for a run. A choice activates the action; a choice is part of your plan. Available choices for the run include what shoes to wear, whether to stretch, where to run, how hard to run, and how long to run.

Some key questions related to your ability to accept responsibility for the run may be: What do you want to accomplish? Why do you want to accomplish this? What is your plan? Will you stick to your plan?

By answering these questions you maintain your clarity regarding your decision to run. By following through on your decision to run, you are conditioning yourself to make the right choice, to be committed. Building commitment involves clarity as to why you want (what you've decided to do), and maintaining a consistent work ethic. The hard work reinforces the conditioning process and provides the learning essential to complete the HiLevel process.

Mental clarity provides the answers to *why* you want to achieve your goals. Mental clarity is determined by the presence of the appropriate neurochemicals (brain chemistry). The abilities to relax, focus and execute are controlled on a physiological level by neurochemicals. Most healthy people are able to control the supply and balance of these essential neurochemicals through their behavior. According to Forest S. Tennant, neurochemicals promote healthy functioning in the following areas:

▲ Attention span, interest and motivation
▲ Muscle tone, eating habits, and the ability to experience pleasure
▲ Reflexes
▲ Natural pain killer
▲ Long and short term memory
▲ Immune system, healing and the control of distress
▲ Endurance
▲ Muscle relaxant & tranquilizer
▲ Mental stability, appetite, sleep control, self-esteem (the ability to be happy).

To enhance the supply and balance of brain chemicals, practice the following behaviors:

**a)** Get some aerobic activity, including deep breathing and moments of extreme motivation.

**b)** Avoid chemicals, especially illicit drugs, alcohol, nicotine, MSG, caffeine, over-the-counter drugs and prescription medications.

**c)** Maintain good attitude. Negative emotions produce adrenaline-like substances which can interfere with the balance of essential brain chemicals.

**d)** Maintain the proper amount of sleep. It is generally accepted that most adults need 8-10 hours of sleep. Dr. James Maas of Cornell suggests that over 60% of the population suffers from permanent "jet lag," due to lack of sleep. Along with the amount of sleep, consistent sleep schedules are said to be important.

**e)** Listen to your favorite music. There are two schools of thought here. One group maintains that the music in question needs to be one beat per second. Others have suggested that any music will do, as long as it is pleasing to you.

**f)** Eat a balanced diet. The key word here is balanced. The most radical advice in this area involves eating special foods that contain "neurotransmitters," foods which directly affect brain function. Fish and fresh fruit are important. Many people prefer low fat diets, avoiding fat around the time of key performances. The decision of what to eat that will allow you to have a balanced diet remains yours. What is certain is that you need to eat. Avoid skipping meals, and work at setting and maintaining regular meal times. The brain seems to thrive on routine.

**g)** Establish and maintain correct weight. Correct weight is loosely defined by Dr. Tennant as being 20 to 30 pounds above or below the accepted standards for height and body type.

**h)** Avoid distress: the negative emotion associated with stress. The research done with the participants in a recent Iditarod dogsled race shows that having realistic expectations and telling yourself the truth about the results of your training is very important.

**i)** Establish and maintain structure in your life. Again, your brain seems to thrive on routine. The establishment of effective structure and a healthy routine also increases the opportunity to experience the pleasure associated with doing what you love.

**j)** Laugh at least five times a day and give and receive several hugs each day. Norman Cousins' work with the importance of laughter and the relationship between positive emotions and the production of endorphins makes these activities a must.

# Light Your Fire

Lighting your fire requires the confidence (the spark) to be mentally tough, the physical and emotional energy or fitness (the fire) to focus and the commitment (the fuel) to follow through.

| MIND | BODY | SPIRIT |
|------|------|--------|
| Confidence | Fitness | Acceptance |
| Mental Toughness | Focus | Follow-Through |
| Belief + Attitude | Thought + Feeling | Decision + Choice |
| Mentally | Physically | Spiritually |
| Your best effort comes when you are confident, when you believe in yourself enough to relax and perform under pressure. | Your best effort comes when you are physically and emotionally ready, when you can "get up and stay up," that is, maintain your physical and emotional intensity and focus. | Your best effort comes when you are willing to accept responsibility for making it happen, able to follow-through, able to make a training schedule and stick to it. |

## Summary

Prepare for each training session, generate positive attitudes and beliefs, participate fully, and work hard. Belief creates experience. Confidence is the spark! Increase your confidence by working to generate positive belief systems.

Fitness is the fire! Increase your fitness, by working to build your physical and emotional conditioning. Work hard, learn how to light a fire as big and as bright as the intensity of your desire.

Maintain your base of physical and emotional fitness, and practice maintaining your focus (state control). Complete each training session, combine clear decisions and the right choices with a consistent work ethic.

Commitment is the fuel! Increase your level of commitment by working to make responsible decisions and appropriate choices.

From now on in the HiLevel process, each step builds on the work accomplished in the previous step. It is important to remember that the steps of getting to HiLevel are the qualities of being there. HiLevel has to do with the journey, not the destination. The work it takes to get to HiLevel, the work gives back to you.

*"From now on in the HiLevel process, each step builds on the work accomplished in the previous step. It is important to remember that the steps of getting to HiLevel are the qualities of being there. HiLevel has to do with the journey, not the destination. The work it takes to get to HiLevel, the work gives back to you."*

My dream is to some day have a HiLevel Performance Clinic, a place where athletes can come to learn about the process of creating PrimeTime. I feel that there is a huge need for such a place, and perhaps the biggest need exists in the population of athletes who have lost their fire, those athletes who no longer feel the passion for their sport and as a result are no longer able to perform up to their standards. I know firsthand the pain that these athletes feel. I lost my fire as a high school wrestler, a college football player, and as a big-wave surfer. When the fire goes out, confusion and anger set in, and, for the most part, the answer seems to be: quit or move on.

For one such lady, Marissa Fry, this was not the case. A "frosh phenom," bursting onto the cross-country scene in her first year of high school, she unfortunately lost her fire. Initially, the track world buzzed with excitement over this girl's future. The first spring she ran a 5:23 mile, a wonderful time that was sure to improve. Her coaches began to dream about her future; her parents began to plan her future. College scholarships and the Olympics were mentioned as strong possibilities. Marissa was enjoying the attention, but not the pressure.

Then, during the final of the State meet, her big hurt came. She was running in first place with a lap to go, when out of nowhere came another girl Marissa had never heard of. The girl blew by Marissa and before she could recover, Marissa was beaten. She was furious: at her coaches for not preparing her, at her parents for putting pressure on her, and at herself for losing.

Marissa's anger festered and soon her fire went out. She no longer ran with the same enthusiasm; in fact, soon she hated running. Her sophomore and junior years were big disappointments. Injuries came and went, but one thing was constant: discussion of what had happened to her fire.

Coming into her senior year, Marissa was determined to get her fire back. Two weeks before the state meet in cross-country, she sprained an ankle. Miraculously she ran in the meet and put up her best race of the season. A spark returned. Heading into track season her determination grew. She began to write and talk about her anger and the frustration that dated back to her freshman year. She began to work on her pre-race anxiety. She began, as she says, "to turn anxiety into excitement." In the final of the State meet in the mile, her spark ignited into flame. She blazed to her personal best, a 5:22 race. The race was a huge win for her. It relit her fire and she loved running again. Best of all, she realized that she had given her best effort. The fact that she had come in second, did not take away from her personal victory. Marissa was back and so was her fire.

When I asked her the secret of her success, she replied, "Throughout my race, I repeated this phrase: allow yourself to do good, relax, and turn nervous into desire. I realized that in the past, I have been my own worst enemy, and finally I have learned to take care of myself and give my best effort." Marissa learned how to relight her fire and create PrimeTime.

n step three, you learned to light your own fire. In step 4, you will learn to maintain the momentum gained from your efforts. Momentum is the energy created when you do well at what you love to do. The feelings related to this energy are a powerful source of motivation. Feelings of enthusiasm, pleasure, satisfaction and joy created when you exercise, resonate throughout your body, enhancing every aspect of your mind, body and spirit. To be aware of these feelings and to express them is to make full use of your emotional intelligence.

# STEP FOUR

## Build momentum by refining your skills.

As Daniel Goleman points out, "To the degree to which we are motivated by feelings of enthusiasm and pleasure in what we do, they propel us to accomplishment." The feelings associated with doing well at what you love are a precious source of fuel that can "propel" you forward, now and in the future. The fuel provides confidence; it feels great and you did it! It turbocharges your fitness, the aliveness that you feel in your muscles. It enhances your commitment; your self-esteem gets a huge stroke leaving you ready to do it again. In the future, this fuel allows you to recreate your best performance on a feeling level.

These feelings must be "pinned" or "anchored." During moments of momentum, your brain records everything that's going on around you—the sounds, the pictures, the smells. Enhancing the recording of these feelings is a skill known as anchoring, a physical movement like a clenched fist that allows you to link the feelings that are present with the movement in question. Imagine the mountain climber going up a familiar piton route. Each physical movement anchors the feelings and the related movements. If repeated often enough, the anchor or piton placement will allow you to recreate the feelings of momentum at will.

During or after moments of momentum, focus on your breathing, relax, and ask yourself two questions: What do I love to do? and, To what is my commitment? The answers to these questions combined with a ritual that includes a physical movement will anchor these feelings.

I remember working with Marty Thomas prior to a major surf meet. Marty had noticed a flaw in his surfing. When he was tired, he came out of his turn too soon and over-extended his body. In this position, he lost power and appeared out of control. To correct this situation, Marty became aware of the feelings he associated with a good, strong turn. He then anchored these feelings, by focusing on the feelings of strength in his legs when they were bent just right. Over and over again he turned and focused on the feelings in his thighs. He anchored these feelings with the form that he wanted to use when he turned off the bottom of a wave. In time, he was able to recreate these feelings and the proper form for turning at will.

For Marty, the answer to the question of what he loved to do was simple: he wanted to be able to consistently turn off the bottom of a wave with strength and style. His commitment was to train his mind, body and spirit to surf with strength and style under pressure in all kinds of conditions. He was able to condition his feelings. Related to specific emotions, such as interest, intensity, excitement, and passion, he was able to link to a sound or word to produce a conditioned response.

As a kid in elementary school I can remember being conditioned to respond to an air-raid warning. Mrs. Bailey, my third grade teacher, got our attention by describing the importance of these air-raid drills in case of attack by enemy planes during the Korean Conflict. Each day we listened to a recording of the siren and then quickly got under our desks, covered our heads with our arms and curled up in a fetal position. On a regular basis, our town sounded the siren and we all practiced our air-raid drill. To this day, whenever I hear that siren, I feel the intensity and picture myself getting in air-raid position. In this case, the stimulus was the air-raid warning and the response was to get in a fetal position under your desk. The conditioned response was to link the siren with the feelings of emotional intensity associated with responding to the drill at once.

As a college football player, I can remember being conditioned as a linebacker to respond to an intercepted pass. As soon as the quarterback showed pass, I was to back-peddle to my spot. As the quarterback pulled up to pass, I was to break on the ball in the direction it was thrown. In the event the ball was intercepted, the call "Oscar" signaled that a run back was in progress. At the sound of "Oscar," I was to break directly up field preparing to block for the player running back the interception, or better yet, I was to intercept the ball and yell "Oscar" at the top of my lungs. Nearly thirty-five years later, my body still knows what to do in response to the call of "Oscar."

Identify the stimulus and response cycle for an important skill. Use a verbal command to condition yourself to respond in an appropriate manner. For example, you are playing volleyball and the ball has been passed to you. You want to be in position to hit the ball with proper form. The verbal command "ball" can be used as a conditioned response for hitting the ball with proper form. The stimulus is your interest to hit the ball correctly and the response is focusing all of your attention on the ball. The command "ball" can condition you to get into position, to focus on the ball and to follow through with good form.

The mental training skills of programming your mind, breathing, relaxing, and thinking in a feeling sense must be combined with feelings you associate with momentum. Doing this can have dramatic effects on your performance. Most people practice these skills naturally in the form of mental rehearsal, psychological reminders, and guided imagery.

To practice these skills on a regular basis facilitates your ability to record feeling memories and to bring up these memories before, during or after your performance to produce a desired state, that is, mentally ready before, excited during, and/or relaxed and accepting after your performance.

## Mental Rehearsal

This skill can be performed with physical involvement, eyes open or closed, and in a variety of settings. Select a skill such as the power jibe or an area of your performance you would like to improve and follow these steps:

1) Break the movement or activity down into a sequence of statements or visions. In the case of the power jibe, it is made up of the following moves: adjust sail, shift weight and start turn, drop back foot and complete turn, shift feet, flip sail, and sheet in (pull in the boom).

2) For each move, identify the focus of your attention, the feelings, the thoughts, the movement of your body, your breathing and your mental state.

**3)** Now identify the most important thoughts, feelings and actions for each move as you complete the entire sequence. Give names or come up with "buzz" words to describe these important thoughts, feelings and actions. For example, "Down" could be used as the most important feeling and action you need to have when completing the turn. "Down" reminds you to keep your weight down, with legs bent and butt down throughout the turn. Saying "Down" to yourself when you're windsurfing, could help you to be in the right position at the critical time.

**4)** Now put the sequence together and mentally and physically rehearse the entire move. Combine sessions of imagining yourself doing the movements with sessions of physically performing the movements. Emphasize the feelings associated with the completion of the move, the feelings that build confidence. For example, when you are working out in the gym, bend your legs in the position of the turn and think and feel "down."

**5)** "Bump it a level," increase the intensity of your performance, imagine mental and physical distractions. Mentally and physically rehearse the completion of the move in the most difficult of situations. "Bumping" it for you could mean going from a jibe in flat water, to jibing in waves—first in small waves, then bigger waves, waves over the reef, and then in waves when the wind stops.

Note that mental rehearsal programs the mind and the body. The feelings that get recorded in the subconscious stimulate the neuromuscular passageways that produce the desired movement, muscle tension, and timing involved in the completion of the skill or skills to be improved. Mental rehearsal has been used successfully in therapies treating disease, overcoming phobias, and managing anger.

## Psychological Reminders

We often use sticky tab notes, memos on the refrigerator, or notes on a calendar as reminders. Psychological reminders are a form of mental rehearsal. They can be used at any time during a workout, performance session, or during the course of your day. A symbol or word can become a "psychological reminder." Looking at the symbol or word can produce a thought about something you want to think, feel and do. The symbol or word can be a reminder for you to have fun, to get serious, or to stay with your program.

Begin by defining what the symbol or word means for you; be specific as to what it is you want to achieve. Write it down, and in the process see it, feel it and practice achieving it in your mind. Be creative: allow the symbol or word to represent you completing this act. Every time you look at the symbol or word, experience the "reminder," the thoughts, feelings and actions associated with your achieving what you want. The more repetitions and intensity of the feelings you associate with the symbol or word, the stronger the reminder will be. Kenny Bradshaw, for example, has the HiLevel logo strategically placed in his shaping room, to remind him to stay focused when shaping.

# The HiLevel Logo

The HiLevel Logo acts as a psychological reminder of what it is you want to achieve. Use it to represent your own choices.

## Guided Imagery

Imagery may include daydreaming, visualizing special moments or special skills, or doodling, drawing pictures of waves, muscles and special events. The skill of "guided imagery" combines deep breathing, relaxation techniques, and mental rehearsal. It involves listening to an audio tape to learn a specific skill or sequence of skills.

The following example of guided imagery will give you a sense of how this skill could work for you:

**1)** Take three deep, relaxed and complete breaths. Sitting or lying down in a comfortable position, close your eyes and involve all of your senses as you look up slightly and imagine seeing a large TV screen.

**2)** Use your imagination to picture a body of water on the screen. Notice the color of the water, notice the texture of the water. Step into the screen. Feel the warmth of the sun, feel the wind as it blows against your face, and smell the fresh air. Imagine you are standing on a stretch of land. The body of water is before you.

3) Step forward slightly and begin to walk towards your body of water. Feel the contact that your feet make with the surface beneath your feet. As you approach the water, walk slowly to the edge, look down and see your reflection in the water; the skin of your face appears smooth and you appear confident and relaxed. . . your body is healthy and relaxed, very healthy and relaxed.

4) Bend down and pick up a rock. Feel the contact of the rock as you hold the rock in your hand. Now pull back your arm and throw the rock out into the water. As the rock lands in the water, it makes a large splash, sending ripples of energy out from the splash. As the ripples move out from the splash, the energy dissipates and the water becomes calm. As you watch the water become calm, you notice that you are getting more and more relaxed.. Open your eyes and notice if you feel more relaxed. With practice this exercise can produce the same results when performed with your eyes open.

Note that you can write the script for your ideal performance and make your own audio recording, or purchase a tape that covers a topic that appeals to you. As with any skill, the more you listen and the more you get involved in listening to the tape, the better the results.

These skills of anchoring and conditioning positive feelings, mental rehearsal, psychological reminders and guided imagery make full use of what Goleman refers to as your emotional intelligence. These skills also present a perfect example of how hard work can contribute to your over- all well-being. When practiced on a regular basis these skills can:

1) Increase blood flow to the brain.

2) Produce a relaxed state which increases the production of the brain chemical serotonin (linked with mental stability, sleep control, appetite, self-esteem).

3) Satisfy the strongest emotional and psychological drive, the need to express creativity.

In the late '70s, the husband-wife team of Doctors Carl and Amy Simmonton brought the concept of mental training into the main stream with their work with cancer patients. The Simmontons held the belief that cancer patients could put their cancer into remission with the use

# Karch K = Momentum

Considered by most people to be the best volleyball player in the world, Karch Kiraly has his own system for maintaining momentum. He simply outworks everybody in his sport. For four months a year he trains as follows:

1) three days a week of beach volleyball
2) one day of plyometrics
3) one day of movement training
4) four days of power lifting with free weights.

Especially noteworthy in his training sessions is the intensity with which he trains, the height and power of his jump and the amount of weight he lifts.

He is intense. He does not talk or rest between sets and he often trains to exhaustion, that is, three hundred fifty net jumps wearing a fifteen-pound weight belt.

There is height to and power in his jump. At the age of thirty-five he has a forty-inch plus vertical jump. His jumping routine includes four sets of twelve repetitions of jumping up on a bench with a thirty-pound dumbbell in each hand.

He balances the amount of weight he lifts. He starts his squat routine at two hundred twenty-five pounds, works up to four reps with five hundred pounds and finishes with sixteen reps at three hundred sixty-five pounds.

It's no wonder his friends refer to him as an "animal." Karch is motivated by the enthusiasm he has for his training and the love he has for his sport.

of exercise, diet and mental training. The mental training they employed included an exercise where the cancer patients were taught to imagine that a war was going on in their bodies. The cancer cells were the bad guys all dressed in black, while the white cells were the good guys, naturally dressed in white. Each day the patients were to visualize this war in complete detail with the white cells inflicting huge losses on the bad-cancer cells. This exercise was given a lot of press as many of the Simmonton patients' cancers went into remission. While the role that this exercise played in the lives of these patients has been debated for some time, the notion that you can participate as a patient in your own recovery is alive and well. A modern day version does exist.

In preparing for surgery on my neck in March of '95, Doctor Bruce Eliashof gave me the following exercise. I was to spend 20 minutes, twice each day listening to my favorite music. During these sessions I was to create the best feeling in my body possible. I imagined and felt the feeling of coming out of the water after a perfect day of windsurfing at Diamond Head.

Along with this feeling, I was to imagine the work of the osteoblast and osteoclast cells. My operation was to help achieve a fusion of two bones and these two sets of cells needed to perform vital functions. The osteoblast cells are a resin-like material that comes and glues the bones together and the osteoclast cells come and sand down the edges of the fusion.

While I have no scientific data to show that my mental work played a role in the success of my operation, I do know that I looked forward to those sessions and that they made me feel better. Most of all, I wanted to know that I was participating in my recovery and my efforts allowed me to feel that I was.

In the creation of PrimeTime, anchoring, mental rehearsal, psychological reminders, and guided imagery are skills used to increase your belief in yourself; amplify your feelings of interest, intensity, excitement, and passion; and solidify your ability to make the right choices. A host of "R" words can be employed in this process. For example, Karch has used hard work to *reinforce* his belief that he is a superior athlete.

The "R" words, techniques for increasing your ability to focus, can be applied in all areas of your life. Clint Eastwood makes use of an "R" word as he describes his ability to focus. "You have to pull that emotion from deep down inside yourself. So you're constantly taking little *reminders* of yourself and placing them into various roles."

Other key "R" words include:

*Record* to pause after the completion of a desired action and focus on the feelings related to doing it right.

*Remember* to focus on important thoughts, feelings and actions before, during and after your performance.

*Replay* to enhance your learning, evaluate your performance and imagine making the desired corrections.

*Revitalize* to change gears, pick up the pace and increase your fire.

*Recreate* to contemplate your best effort and pull it off.

*Rejoice* to celebrate your effort and/or the completion of a particular skill.

*Redo* to edit your performance, make mental corrections and practice doing these skills right.

*Reframe* to turn a negative thought, feeling or action into a positive learning experience.

*Recognize* to gain critical awareness.

In step four, you learned how to maintain the momentum gained from your efforts. In step five, you will learn how to refine your focus. As discussed earlier, to focus is to concentrate all of your energy on seeing an object, making a decision, performing a task, and/or maintaining a specific feeling or emotional state. To refine your focus you must strengthen your commitment to create and increase your mental clarity, physical strength and endurance, emotional intensity, and spiritual presence.

# STEP FIVE

# Focus your awareness and commitment

This will put you in position to give your best effort. You will know what to do mentally and be able to accomplish it. You will have the emotional fire for doing it. And you will be fully involved in doing it spiritually.

As it relates to performance, awareness is defined as a working knowledge of what is required to accomplish what you want in light of personal assets such as sleep and possible distractions such as anger or fear. A working knowledge tells you how much mental, physical, emotional and spiritual energy you need. It amounts to information that, as Deepak Chopra says, gives you options: "Reactions result in a closed set of options, awareness results in an open set of options."

Choosing one of the options provided by this information is the work of commitment, taking responsibility for your actions. To prepare is to decide how you are going to create the energy, given your options. To execute is to make the right choice that results in an increase in energy.

As Csikszentmihalyi says, when "action and awareness merge. . . there [is] one-pointedness of mind." This is what makes being committed a spiritual matter. Your actions represent the strength of your spirit. To make a decision and then to act accordingly is to be true to yourself.

There are two basic ways to create the energy you need for refining your focus: 1) Manage the downtime in your performance and in your life, that is, learn to rest during your activity and take really good care of yourself in general. 2) Control your emotions, that is, increase your positive emotions and decrease your negative emotions.

## DownTime Management

DownTime is a pause in the action, a time when you can rest your mind, your body, your emotions and your spirit. Downtime management is the ability to choose to use this time wisely: to relax, to rest, to refocus, to generate positive thoughts and feelings, and to make really smart decisions. Depending on your activity, there may be times when you can rest partially, completely, or not at all.

You may rest *partially* in a swimming race when you push off the wall in a turn and your shoulders get a rest. You may rest *completely* during a time-out in basketball when your whole "self" gets a rest. You may have *no rest* when running out for a pass in football.

Downtime is an opportunity to refine your focus, to increase your clarity, to restore your strength and endurance, to rebuild your fire, to reestablish your faith. There is good downtime, bad downtime, and forced downtime. Good downtime is an opportunity to increase your focus, bad downtime is a loss of focus, and forced downtime is an opportunity to recover your focus.

Good downtime provides for preparation, timeout, and transition, the time between sessions, workouts or competitions where you manage your time and energy really well. You eat right, drink plenty of water, stretch, or relax, and get a good night's sleep.

A timeout is a rest during a session, workout or competition, such as a rest on the beach relaxing and drinking fluids when windsurfing, the time in between "sets" when you are lifting weights, or a twenty-second rest period during a basketball game. Transitions are moments of relaxation or a shift in focus during sessions, workouts or competitions, basically the times between sets of waves when you are surfing, the times in between reps when you are lifting weights, or between pitches in a baseball game.

Bad downtime is sometimes referred to as phase-out, or off-air, a loss of focus during the course of a session, workout or competition such as when your mind wanders and you miss a wave, when you neglect to use good form lifting weights, or when you get distracted by the crowd during your basketball game.

Forced downtime may involve rehab, time when you are out of action due to an illness or injury. Downtime management here will allow you to learn from the situation and return to the action feeling rested and rejuvenated.

It is very important in downtime to be smart. Identify distractions, those decisions which have consequences inconsistent with what you want, such as staying up late when you want to be asleep, drinking alcohol or using illegal drugs when you want to be clean and sober. Creatively continue to find ways to take advantage of the downtime that is available to you. Consistently establish rituals and plans for action based on what works for you.

Downtime management is the ability to plan wisely and then to have the discipline and maturity to avoid distractions, control your emotions, and carry out your plan. In the case of the time during sessions, workouts or competitions, the essence of downtime management is contained in the following four steps:

**1)** Recognize the presence of downtime; confront the reality of your situation and plan accordingly. Celebrate physically. Consider a verbal command like, "Yes!" and then clench your fist. Positive action helps record good feelings and reframes negative feelings. Clear your mind. Take a few deep breaths, relax and stretch. If you are unable to relax or effectively reframe negative feelings, take a break, rest, or call it a day.

**2)** Communicate with yourself or teammates. Affirm your ability and work on your attitude. Communication on an individual basis that allows you to affirm your ability and work on your attitude is known as positive self-talk and/or talking nice to yourself. Talk nice to yourself as you review what happened, replay and rehearse what you wanted to have happen, check feelings, and affirm your ability. Say, "Yes, I (we) can do this!" Communication on a group or team basis that allows everyone involved to affirm their abilities and work on their attitudes is known as making emotional deposits. Listen to what is being said by your coach, captain or training partner; think in a feeling sense as you mentally rehearse the information that relates to you and your performance.

**3)** Focus on recording what you have learned and prepare mentally to return to the action. Relax and take a few deep breaths. Remind yourself of where you are and what you want to accomplish.

Take another deep breath; see and feel what you plan to do.

**4)** Light your own fire. This will allow you to get back into the action with vigor. Affirm your fire. Express your confidence. Focus on the appropriate emotional state and see and feel what you plan to do and act the part.

Throughout this four-step process, generate positive thoughts, feelings, facial expressions, and body posture. These positive behaviors send chemical messages to your brain that enhance your ability to relax, refocus and create positive energy.

Downtime management is one of the most important tools of the HiLevel process. Your ability here will affect both your life and your athletic performance. Be creative, find a way to create the energy you need to refine your focus, and your performance will improve and you will have more fun.

Consider the case of tennis. During match play, the rest-to-work ratio is one-to-two; for every one second of work there are two seconds of rest. In the Men's Final at Wimbledon in 1991, in a match between Michael Stich and Boris Becker, the average point took 2.6 seconds. For every hour they played, they had 56 minutes of downtime and 4 minutes of play time. In the Men's Finals at the French Open in 1991, in a match between Andre Agassi and Jim Courier, the average point took 10 seconds. The French Open is played on clay, a much slower surface. For each hour they played they had 46 minutes of downtime and 14 minutes of play time. In each case, the player who did the best job of managing this substantial amount of downtime, had a definite advantage.

## Emotional Control

For HiLevel performance you need positive energy: interest, intensity, excitement, and passion. When you have these they eliminate or modify your pain, fear, and anger. Negative emotions can be refocused, put on the back burner, and/or reframed into positive energy. Feelings of frustration can be redirected by establishing more realistic expectations.

The reframe process involves learning how to recognize and process negative emotions, to change your attitude and to turn negative energy into positive energy. Begin the process by defining your issue and be sure to identify your feelings related to this issue.

Answering the following five questions will allow you to be clear about what is upsetting you, and to focus on the solution to your issue.

The questions are all written as if you are about to reframe this issue. This is to help you get into a solution mode, rather than a victim mode.

You must want to reframe the issue with questions. If you have trouble answering the questions and completing the process, perhaps you are not ready.

Somewhere in the exercise, perhaps around questions 3 and 4, you will feel a "letting go" of the negative feelings. Again, if you don't experience this letting go, maybe you are not ready and/or you need to repeat the process.

The final question is the hardest for most people. To help you to focus on your pride, think about how good you will feel about yourself when you have reframed this issue.

In psychological terms, the reframe process is a form of proactive behavior, proactive in that you are able to step outside yourself and evaluate your behavior, consider your options, and then decide to change your attitude and behavior based on your principles. In the heat of the moment, this exercise may seem like a real stretch. Remember to reserve judgment and be patient with yourself.

**1)** What are the positive aspects of this issue?

**2)** What is the upset related to this issue?

**3)** What am I eager to do to resolve this issue?

**4)** What will be my focus in resolving this issue?

**5)** How can I take pride in my ability to reframe this issue?

A word must be said about pain, fear and anger. The presence of pain can be an important message from your body that: a) you are approaching the limit of your strength and endurance; b) you have reached the limit of your strength and endurance; c) you are out of gas, sick or injured.

In all three cases, there are times when you can reframe this pain, push the limits of your pain threshold, and keep going. There are also times when you would be smart to stop or back off. Recognizing the difference is a product of your awareness, that is, what have you learned to date about the presence of this pain, and what your commitment is. Are you eager to continue or stop and maintain your health and/or safety?

Meredith Rainey, winner of the 1996 U.S. Olympic Trials in the 800 meters, seems to have mastered the ability to handle the pain associated with her event. "If you want to excel, you'll have to learn to endure pain. To reach the next level, you have to expect some pain. Welcome it, manage it. You can't fear pain."

The presence of fear may be a message signaling that 1) you are in danger (a shark is swimming through the area where you are windsurfing); 2) you are operating outside your comfort zone (perhaps competing against someone much bigger, stronger, and better than you and you don't want to be hurt or embarrassed); or 3) you have conditioned yourself to associate fear with the process of getting ready and/or being ready (the nervous feeling in your stomach before a big game).

In all three cases, your fear can be reframed. The question is: when is your fear a source of energy that when reframed can be used to enhance your performance? Fear of speaking to large groups can be energizing.

When I first started speaking to large groups of people, I was afraid beyond belief. Gradually, I learned to manage my fear, firstly, by associating it with a signal that I was ready, and, secondly, by using it as a reminder of how much I cared about what I was about to do.

Over the years, I got to the point where I was too relaxed and I appeared to be disinterested or aloof. On receiving this feedback from myself and others, I went back to allowing myself to be afraid, just enough to feel energized at the beginning of a talk. As I begin my talks today, I still work on finding the right balance between fear and relaxation.

Fear can also warn of possible serious injury. Just recently I grew afraid as I entered the water to windsurf. I was pushing the limits. Actually, I was being stupid. I was about to windsurf on a day when I had a severely bruised and sprained hand. Earlier in the day, I had taken a serious fall on my mountain bike. My right hand was swollen and extremely painful. Instead of listening to my fear, I taped up my hand and went for it, showing poor judgment. I was unable to sail well. I didn't have fun. I added to the seriousness of the injury and increased the length of my rehab.

The presence of anger is a clear message that you are upset at yourself or the actions of another. Related to making performance mistakes, it is evidence of how much you care. The reason for the anger, however, can be reframed to enhance your learning. When you reframe and articulate your anger instead of venting it on someone, you give it clarity and a possible automatic release. If you do this successfully you will add to your self-esteem.

The presence of anger is always a message that needs to be taken seriously. Perhaps it really is a signal that you are afraid, embarrassed, or that your feelings are hurt. Your anger indicates that certain actions of others have some importance to you. If they didn't, you wouldn't be upset. The more upset you are at the actions of others, the more you need to reframe this issue and the more this issue has to teach you about yourself.

In the case where you are angry and your anger is counter-productive to your performance, you need to develop the mental toughness and follow-through to refocus your anger instantly. In the words of Peter Balding, "Put your anger on the back burner."

When frustrated and "stuck" with feelings that are wearing you down, consider breaking what it is you want to accomplish into smaller increments. Perhaps you have taken on too much.

The refocus process involves training your mind to break the cause-and-effect cycle that accompanies emotional upsets. Trigger words are used to command yourself to refocus, to put your anger on hold.

Imagine that you are angry at someone or something and the anger represents a distraction to your ability to give your best effort. The trigger word Stop could be used to command yourself to refocus your anger and refocus instead on a positive feeling related to your performance. The idea is to use the words that work best for you and to associate these words with positive thoughts, feelings, and actions .

Note that the skill of refocusing is closely related to the defense mechanism of denial or repression, where negative thoughts and feelings are ignored or forcefully pushed aside. To prevent the practice of an unhealthy behavior, you need to reframe your anger at an appropriate time. Reframing it will allow you to get rid of this negative energy and learn from your experience.

At the same time, you must beware of false fatigue. Mental training techniques can effectively reframe or refocus the fear or pain that accompanies "false fatigue," the feelings of physical fatigue caused prematurely by your emotions. False fatigue can be the feeling of being exhausted prior to paddling out in big surf, the burning in your shoulders as you "think too far ahead" in a paddling race, the heaviness in your legs as you start to run or pedal up a hill, or the accelerated breathing that goes with the negative emotions of fear and anger.

Once again, there may be times when this exercise may seem like a real stretch. Remember to reserve judgment and be patient with yourself.

# Refine Your Focus

## The Top 10 Coaching Points

1) **Get Plenty of Rest** The human-to-car analogy works here. Rest is your battery and the ability to focus is your headlights. Maintain your rest and your battery is fully charged and your lights are bright. Operate without rest and your batteries run down and your lights flicker and go dim.

2) **Take Power Naps** Listen to the PrimeTime tape (available from HiLevel Productions, P.O. Box 61866, Honolulu, Hawaii 96839), sides 1 and 2, as a part of your downtime management. Consider listening to side 1 first thing in the morning and/or at some point during your day, and side 2 right before you go to bed. Listening to this tape will assist with your preparation and increase the quality of your sleep.

3) **Eat on Time** The human body seems to thrive on a diet of 4 or 5 small meals per day. What to eat and when to eat continues to be an individual matter. Establish the best diet and the best times to eat and stick to it. Your diet should add to your ability to focus, not make you sleepy and/or ready for bed.

4) **Hyper-hydrate** Drink plenty of water each day. Fluids are critical to a healthy mind and body. Consider that one of the early warning signs of dehydration is lack of clarity. Make it a point to drink water throughout your activity and notice the difference in your ability to focus.

5) **Be Still and Clear Your Mind** Practice taking a deep breath, let it out slowly and command yourself to relax. Focus on a color, a peaceful scene, or an affirmation, and allow your mind to be quiet. Practice this technique throughout your day, especially before making important decisions and/or communications. The idea is to establish a routine that allows you to focus at your very best.

**6) Express Your Fire** Make what you are doing each moment the most important thing and feel the interest, intensity, excitement, and passion. The idea is to condition yourself to practice as you want to play and to focus at your very best under pressure and for long periods of time.

**7) Release Tension** Relax your mind and stretch your body. The idea is to release any physical tension caused by muscle strain and/or a build-up of lactic acid. Shiatsu and athletic massage are most helpful in this regard. The tension in your neck and shoulders that can cause headaches also restricts the flow of blood to your brain. To refine your focus, make sure your muscles and your brain are receiving the oxygen required to function properly.

**8) Hoot and Heal** To hoot is to forcefully expel negative emotions and to heal is to apologize and to make amends for your actions. Both of these behaviors serve to release your stress and make it easier to focus in present time. Toxic emotions that are allowed to fester not only interfere with your ability to focus, they take away from your ability to be objective.

**9) Connect with Nature** Take a walk, go for a swim, breathe some fresh air, smell the flowers, watch a sunset. Make an effort to visit the places that talk to your spirit and nourish your soul. The additional clarity gained during this special downtime can help you see the big picture, including the available options.

**10) Pray** Acknowledge the source of your strength and focus on the feelings related to the relationship you have with this source of strength. Faith in yourself and in your spiritual beliefs is the essence of the ability to focus.

## The Bigger Picture

The ability to manage downtime and control your emotions (reframe, refocus and redirect) are skills that can be applied in all areas of your life. These skills require a delicate balance between awareness and commitment. Phil Jackson, in his book *Sacred Hoops,* offers two examples which point out the balance between downtime management and emotional control for basketball players.

Downtime management: "During the fifteen or thirty seconds they have to grab a drink or towel off, I encourage them to picture themselves someplace where they feel secure. It's a way for them to take a short mental vacation before addressing the problem at hand."

Emotional control: "If somebody fouled them hard, I suggested turning around, taking a deep breath, and staying as composed as possible so they could keep their minds fixed on our goal: victory."

In both cases, there is an element of downtime management and emotional control. To create a "safe spot" during a time-out requires the control to relax and rest and the control to block out the excitement of the game. To walk away from a physical confrontation requires the control to see that you have a choice and the control to keep walking. Whenever you have a difficult decision to make you want equal parts awareness and commitment: the awareness to know your options and the commitment to make the decision that is right for you.

## PrimeTime Wrap

As the Kenny Rogers song goes, ". . . know when to hold 'em and know when to fold 'em." To refine your focus is to know when to hold 'em and when to fold 'em. Simply put, to be effective you need to know when to push your limits and when to pull back and play it safe, when to work hard and when to rest, and when to rely on yourself and when to ask for help. In Habit 7 in his book, *The 7 Habits of Highly Effective People*, Stephen Covey says it is important to take the time to sharpen the saw. For Covey, this has to do with preserving and enhancing your greatest asset: you. In my example, the need to work hard is represented by the column "hold 'em" and the need to rest is represented by the column "fold 'em."

|  | Hold 'em | Fold 'em |
|---|---|---|
| **Mental Toughness:** | Push through your fear. | Know your limits. |
| **Focus:** | Push through the pain. | Take a day off. |
| **Commitment:** | Do it yourself. | Ask for help. |

When you are "aware" you know when to hold 'em and when to fold 'em. When you act on this awareness you are being true to your commitment. I asked Robby Naish how he knows when it's time to "bail out" and he said, "I think it's time to bail whenever the conditions are too much to handle. I really enjoy living and I especially want to be able to sail tomorrow. I don't see myself as a hero. I've been injured and I don't like going through the forced downtime. I may have a lower threshold of discomfort than some people, but whenever it begins to feel stupid. . . I bail. My focus is to have fun and when the fun stops I go in. Better safe than sorry. . . at this point in my career I prefer to be safe."

In step five, you learned how to refine your focus. In step six, you will learn how to build trust. Trust is the quality that allows you to know — absolutely — that you can create PrimeTime: that you have the skills to perform at that level, that you can relax under pressure and give your best effort and expect to do well. Goethe once said something I like to quote to my students: "Just trust in yourself and you will know how to live."

Robby Naish performs at the level of trust and he generates this feeling when he windsurfs. For fifteen years I have seen Robby sail harder and longer than anyone else at Diamond Head. I have seen him make up moves on the spur of the moment that cause even

# STEP SIX

# Build trust in yourself and your performance level.

the best sailors to pause and wonder. For example, I was sailing out one day, on perhaps the best day ever at Diamond Head, when Naish caught a wave at Dudgeon reef. He was headed straight for me on a large, thick left that began to throw out. I scurried to make it over the wave in question and get out of his way. As I looked down the barrel of the wave, Naish was at a point where I was sure he would turn down the face. Instead, he jammed a turn up into the lip with such force I was truly concerned for his judgment and well-being.

When I turned to see if he had made the wave, Naish was nowhere in sight. About ten minutes later Naish was back in the lineup with a big smile on his face. When I asked him if he had made the wave, much to my amazement he said, "Yes, but the lip of the wave broke my boom." In the ten minutes that Naish was out of sight, he had sailed in and changed his boom and was now back in the lineup. The trust that Naish has in his ability allows him to sail with incredible intensity, to put himself in critical situations, to pull off moves beyond astonishing and to endure the most intense rigors of windsurfing at this level.

The level of trust you will need in yourself and in your skills to create PrimeTime is dependent on whether you view yourself as a participant, HiLevel Participant, competitor, or a HiLevel Competitor.

As a "participant," by definition you are taking part in an activity for purposes of recreation, fellowship, and/or fun. In a word, you are there for the *experience*. You may or may not have the skills or the conditioning required, your performance may range from poor to good, sporadic to consistent, and requires very little trust. You may play in a pick-up basketball game, weekend softball, or touch football. You stretch before competing, but your workouts are more fitness-related than sport or activity specific. You don't train for your sport, but you do try to stay fit. You play within your limits.

As a "HiLevel participant," by definition, you feel good about your present level of involvement and in this sense you are comfortable with: 1) your skill and performance level, that is, you are happy with your game; 2) the intensity of your workouts and your performances, that is, you recover quickly before, during, and after performances; and 3) the risks inherent in your activity such as the fear of injury and/or forced downtime due to soreness, sickness or fatigue, that is, you play in a pick-up basketball game, you play regularly, you are in shape, and you are playing within your limits.

The operative word regarding participation is *comfortable*, hence, the term "comfort zone." Participating at HiLevel requires you to maintain trust in yourself, your skills, and your skill level (you practice regularly), conditioning, (you maintain a well-defined training regimen), and safety (you perform within your comfort zone at all times).

As a "competitor," by definition, you take part in an activity because you want to win and/or be the best. In a word, you are there for the *challenge*. You may or may not have the skills or the conditioning required; your performance can range from poor to good, sporadic to consistent. It requires a great deal of trust. In other words, you train on a regular basis, but you only take it seriously prior to the marathon or just before the 100k bike race. You have missed competitions due to injury and recovered slowly because you had no formal plan for managing downtime. You have unrealistic expectations that often drive you to great things, but also can lead to injury or unnecessary risks.

As a "HiLevel competitor" you want to "bump" your level of involvement to the next level. In this sense you are eager to: 1) improve your skills and your performance level (eager to move up to the next level of competition); 2) increase the intensity of your workouts and your performances (you are eager to train and perform at your maximum aerobic and anaerobic thresholds); and 3) push your physical and emotional limits, thereby increasing the risks. Forced downtime is due to injuries, soreness, sickness and/or fatigue. It is part of the price you are willing to pay to get better. You play in a pick-up basketball game with some really good players, you are ready, you are in shape and you feel good about pushing your limits.

The operative word regarding competition is risk. As a competitor you are eager to increase the emotional and physical risks inherent in operating outside of your comfort zone. Competing at HiLevel requires a delicate balance between the amount of trust you have in yourself and your abilities and how far you want to push your limits.

Robby Naish is a HiLevel competitor in every sense of the word. He is constantly working to improve his skills and increase the level of his performance, to increase the level of his intensity, and to push his limits.

In terms of trust, to participate or compete at HiLevel you need to be eager to: **1)** set realistic expectations, **2)** work hard, **3)** maintain your fire, **4)** stay present, **5)** stay in the groove, **6)** turn your commitment into expectation, and **7)** accept the results of your actions.

## 1) Realistic Expectations:

The ability to set realistic expectations is critical to your ability to establish and maintain trust in yourself and your ability. Should you set your expectations too high, you set yourself up to lose, and to experience a host of negative emotions ranging from frustration and guilt, to anger and humiliation. Negative emotions destroy trust, erode your fitness level, and create doubt and fear. Conversely, setting your expectations too low will lead to boredom and lack of the creative tension needed to get your full attention.

As a HiLevel Participant you need to be clear about your desire to participate and set your expectations accordingly. During the "fun" of your activity it is easy to get carried away and to be drawn into the competition. The danger here is the injury that could happen when you exceed your comfort zone. For example, I consider myself a HiLevel participant in the weight room, yet it's very easy for me to jump into a competition to see who can do the most reps. If I haven't been training in a particular exercise or the competition exceeds what is smart for me, I run the risk of hurting myself.

As a HiLevel Competitor you need to monitor your readiness; you need to make sure you are up for the challenge and risk. Given the level of intensity and risk, you want to avoid competing when you are tired, sick, or distracted.

It is important to be truthful with yourself about your levels. In his video, "Achieve More With Better Brain Chemistry," Dr. Forest Tennant asserts that setting realistic goals and telling yourself the truth about your results is one of the top ten ideal behaviors for enhancing the supply and balance of brain chemicals.

# Set Realistic Goals

The research to support Dr. Forest Tennant's position was done by the United States Army, which did a study with the competitors in the Iditarod dogsled race. They broke down the contestants into the top-half and bottom-half in accordance with how they finished the grueling race. They tested both groups in terms of their physical and emotional fitness. The physical tests showed very little difference in the physical training of the two groups; however, the top-half had a much higher level of overall fitness. A battery of psychological tests pointed out the cause of this difference.

The top finishers tended to set realistic goals for themselves. The bottom half tended to set unrealistic goals for themselves and they compounded the situation by falsifying their results. The Army reasoned that the combination of unrealistic expectations and the guilt associated with making false statements resulted in feelings of distress and the production of harmful adrenaline-based neurochemicals. The presence of these harmful neurochemicals took away from the overall fitness of the bottom-half finishers.

To establish and maintain trust, continue to set realistic expectations for yourself. Setting realistic expectations and telling yourself the truth is the equivalent of playing win/win with yourself. Review the Coaching Points in Step 1. in the section on creating your own reality.

Note that Bob Goldman asked the following question to a group of Olympic Athletes: "You are offered a banned performance-enhancing substance that comes with two guarantees: a) You will not be caught; b) You will win every competition you enter for the next five years, and then you will die from the side effects of the substance. Would you take it?" More than half the athletes said yes. Apparently the athletes who answered yes have lost the ability to set realistic expectations.

## 2) Work Hard.

Make it nice for yourself; work hard to accomplish a task that is realistic for you. In the process of learning to create PrimeTime, hard work and trust go hand in hand. Hard work is always central to feeling good about your ability to give your best effort.

Mentally, hard work will allow you to believe in yourself to the point where you are able to relax and perform under pressure.

Physically, hard work will allow you to get up and stay up and to maintain your emotional intensity and focus.

Spiritually, hard work will allow you to have faith in your ability to follow through, to show up eager to get the job done.

As a HiLevel Participant, how hard you work will be determined by the time and energy you have for your activity, that is, what makes sense given your lifestyle.

As a HiLevel Competitor, how hard you work will be determined by your ability to push yourself physically and emotionally, that is, what makes sense given your skill level and conditioning. You will probably want a coach or a source of feedback to let you know how you are doing, a training partner for support and safety, and a system for measuring your progress.

For Maui Meyer, a former professional windsurfer, hard work enabled him to overcome a childhood accident. At the age of ten, Meyer was hit by a truck as he walked down the street in Kailua. Left with broken bones in all parts of his body, he was put back together with pins and plates and put in a full body cast for one year. After Meyer was told he would never walk again, his family rallied to his aid. His father made him a skateboard-like device that allowed him to move himself and his cast around the house. His mother made a ritual out of every meal, feeding Meyer the best possible diet. His six older sisters shared in giving Meyer all of the love and support possible.

In this environment his body healed, his mind expanded and his attitude formed. He worked nonstop to overcome his handicap and to keep up with his studies. At the end of one year he was allowed to return to school. He was promoted a grade and put on a restricted schedule of absolutely no sports. One year later the doctor, amazed by Meyer's recovery, suggested windsurfing as a low-impact sport.

In the beginning windsurfing was low-impact, with huge boards and relatively small sails. The doctor in question had no way of knowing that Meyer would help to change the nature of the sport.

Meyer's story is about building trust through hard work, courage and determination. The relevance of his story lies in the fact that he learned to trust in abilities that in the beginning of his rehab he didn't have. His ever-present confidence and trust comes out of an experience that was so severe and an environment that was so loving and supportive that it spawned the birth of his "yes, I know what I want and I can do it" attitude.

Meyer made a contribution to windsurfing on his own terms, received an exceptional education from Cornell University, and combined the two to create his present lifestyle. His life revolves around the work he loves, owning and operating a restaurant, and the sports he loves, kayaking and snowboarding. The decisions he makes on a daily basis reflect his belief in himself and his ability to get the job done.

Maui Meyer is a HiLevel competitor who lives in Hood River, Oregon to be close to the sports he loves. He continues to work and play hard. Describing his ideal summer day and his ideal winter day, Maui says,

*"Most of my time is spent working in the restaurant. However, my ideal summer day goes like this. I do some work on the trampoline. I wear the snowboard on the trampoline to practice my moves. Then I kayak for a few hours. Kayaking involves a four-hour commitment, minimum. Time permitting, I train on two rivers. Then I practice on the rock climbing wall we have here in town or bike ride.*

*"My ideal winter day. I'll be on the mountain by 8:30 and we'll attempt to do 30,000 vertical feet of snowboarding by*

*lunch time. By that time our lower bodies
are shot. In the afternoon we'll go down to
the river. In the winter time the river is
perfect for paddling, the air temperature is
a lot warmer than the water so it is actually quite pleasant, 30 to 40 degrees. I
kayak hard for a couple of hours in the
afternoon. My housemate is a world class
snowboarder, so in the winter we push
each other a lot."*

Make it nice for yourself; learn to enjoy and appreciate the rewards
that come from hard work.

## 3) Maintain Your Fire.

Your eagerness to work hard is directly related to your ability to maintain your fire. . . to have fun and/or see the value of your efforts. While
hard work is what develops trust, your ability to experience the rewards of your efforts is what allows you to keep working hard. As you
move up the steps in the HiLevel process, the ability to define fun and
know what is important to you at all times takes on an added meaning.

As a HiLevel Participant, the fun and/or value for you, by definition,
is part of doing the activity. As a HiLevel Competitor, the fun and/or
value for you is part of the challenge, the effort involved in becoming
better and/or winning.

I asked Pete Cabrinha, age 33, famous for pioneering strap surfing
and doing tow-ins in big waves at Jaws on Maui, how he maintains his
fire for surfing in such big waves.

*"I spend a lot of time getting ready for
surfing at Jaws. I have a boat and I spend
a lot time getting it working right. I skurf
(water-ski with a surfboard) all summer
to stay in tune and by early winter I surf a
lot to get ready for when the big waves
come. I cover my bases. I make sure my
health is good. I wouldn't do it if I was*

*sick. I have no illusions about Jaws. It is a very dangerous place. I know what I'm getting into; if you go down in the wrong spot, a wipe-out can be very serious with all of that water moving around. So I tell myself to take it seriously.*

*"To get psyched up, I think of all of the good rides I've had before and the type of surfing I want to do once I get out there. Once I hear that the surf is hitting the number one buoy on Kauai at fifteen feet at fifteen-second intervals, I know that Jaws will be twelve to eighteen feet and I have a day to get ready, check my board, and make sure all of the straps are secure and my boat is ready. Jaws is an outer reef spot and it is a long boat ride from the harbor. During this long ride, I prepare myself mentally to go out and do well and have fun."*

As a HiLevel Competitor, Pete Cabrinha loves to push the limits of his ability, sail with a style that reflects the trust and confidence that he has in himself and in his ability, and have fun sailing and surfing in big waves in extremely challenging conditions.

When Cabrinha talks about surfing and sailing at Jaws, I can feel the humility and respect that go with building his life around what he really loves to do.

Make it nice for yourself; learn to focus on your feelings related to what you love to do.

Again. Make it nice for yourself; learn to focus on your feelings related to what you love to do.

Absolutely! Make it nice for yourself; learn to focus on your feelings related to what you love to do.

Maintain Your Fire!

# 4) Stay Consciously Present.

To be consciously present is to be thinking and feeling about what is going on right now, that is, to have a present state of awareness. To stay consciously present during your activity is dependent on your ability to relax when you perform, to utilize the breathing and relaxation techniques described in Step 3, to focus on what is happening *right now* and to maintain your interest, intensity, excitement, and passion for your activity. The inability to relax at any time related to your activity is a red flag, a clear warning that you are not operating at the level of trust. The presence of anxiety, negative stress, and fear, by definition, represents the absence of trust. Likewise, feelings of boredom and doubt can indicate a lack of trust. As Goethe said, "Just trust in yourself and you will know how to live."

The ability to stay present during your activity will allow you to be open to receive your instincts, intuitions, and feelings. The knowingness that Goethe describes is the trust to express your feelings in your performance.

As a HiLevel Participant, the challenge for you will be to create the time and energy required to stay consciously present during your activity, that is, to maintain your interest, intensity, excitement, and passion given everything else that is going on in your life.

As a HiLevel Competitor, the challenge for you will be to transcend the pain and discomfort and stay consciously present during your activity, that is, to maintain your interest, intensity, excitement, and passion given the intensity of your workouts and the risk involved in pushing your limits.

When it comes to trust and the ability to stay present there are levels. In the area of natural childbirth there are two techniques which represent different levels of trust.

The Lamaze Technique requires trust in your ability to use breathing as a means of handling the pain of childbirth. In the Lamaze Technique, short and rapid breaths are used as a distraction from the pain and discomfort of the labor contractions and delivery. Certainly, there is more trust required in yourself and in your ability to handle the pain with breathing than to rely on drugs.

However, the Bradley Method requires a much higher level of trust. The Bradley Method uses slow, deep and rhythmic breathing to promote relaxation. While the Lamaze Technique uses breathing as a distraction, the Bradley Method uses breathing as a means for working through the discomfort of labor. The Lamaze Technique, with its rapid and shallow breathing, causes the woman to hyperventilate, tightening the abdomen and intensifying the contractions, whereas the Bradley Method, with its slow and deep breathing, allows the woman to relax, to process the pain and eliminate any physical resistance to delivery.

These two techniques demonstrate the different levels of trust required to stay present during the discomfort of childbirth. To rely on your breathing as a distraction from your pain, requires one level of trust. To rely on your breathing as a way of working with the pain, requires a much higher level of trust. Imagine being in pain, and just when you want to scream and clench your teeth, you take a deep breath, relax and welcome the pain! And. . . you relax and. . . you manage your pain!

Make it nice for yourself, learn to relax and focus on what is happening *right now* during your activity.

## 5) Stay in the Groove.

Staying present is to the mind as staying in the groove is to the body. While staying present allows you to control your mind and your emotions, staying in the groove allows you to control the movement of your body. Staying in the groove is the ability to maintain good form and proper technique, to get into the flow, to feel connected with your activity and to work efficiently. Staying in the groove is closely related to the ability to focus; it demands the physical and emotional conditioning to feel strong throughout your event.

As a HiLevel Participant, the challenge for you will be to show up feeling rested and ready, that is, to maintain your physical and emotional strength throughout your activity.

As a HiLevel Competitor, the challenge for you will be to maintain your conditioning throughout the rigors of your training, that is, to feel strong rather than tired or "burned out."

For Peter Trombly, staying in the groove has to do with maintaining speed and position on the wave when windsurfing at Back Yards. When the waves are twelve to fifteen feet with strong north winds, the challenge in these conditions is to ride a wave for as long as a half-mile with the wave breaking away from the direction you are headed. In such situations, the wave actually appears to be bending away from you.

Says Peter,

> *"I'm amazed at how excited I get when I*
> *sail in these conditions. I've had waves*
> *where I'm challenging the wave from so*

*far back, and the wave is bending away
from me to where I can't see what I'm
doing. I've made outrageous waves like
this by trusting myself to stay high in the
wave, maintain my speed and know that I
can tap into the harmony of the speed of
the wave and the cooperation of the wind
with the face of the wave. On the other
hand, if I lose my confidence, hesitate and
drop down in the wave, I'm history, I don't
make the wave and I'm in for a long
swim."*

Being up for the challenge and staying high in the wave is staying in the groove for Peter Trombly.

Make it nice for yourself, learn to focus on the feelings of interest, intensity, excitement and passion as you perform well.

## 6) Turn Your Commitment into an Expectation.

Revisiting Shakespeare's assumptive attitude I am also reminded of a quote from Goethe, "What you can do, or dream you can, begin it. Boldness has genius, power and magic in it."

The "power" here is a reward for maintaining long-term commitment. It has to do with the feeling of "expecting it to happen." This expectation goes beyond the cocky, self-assured "in your face" attitude that some athletes carry around like a lot of heavy baggage. The attitude that goes with "expecting" a certain result is one of strength and humility. At this level of trust you, like Maui, have learned to trust completely in your ability. Your actions in this state of trust are calm and relaxed. Hard work has brought you to the place where you are very comfortable with yourself and your ability. The hard work is what produces emotional and physical expectation.

As a HiLevel Participant, the challenge for you will be to condition yourself to want to work hard, that is, to associate hard work with fun.

As a HiLevel Competitor, the challenge for you will be to condition yourself to want to push your limits, that is, to associate the pain and discomfort of working this hard with the process of getting better.

Operating at the level of trust releases the power of the human brain to create outcomes, a response known as the placebo effect. Thanks to the contribution of the medical model of psychology, we have well-documented studies on the placebo effect, the power of what Bernie Siegel calls "effective beliefs."

The example he cites in his book, *Love, Medicine & Miracles,* has to do with a cancer patient who believed she could go through chemotherapy without any negative side effects. She held onto the image that her chemotherapy was "scrubbing bubbles from a TV commercial for a bathroom cleanser. She never had any significant adverse reactions."

David Bresler in his book, *Free Yourself from Pain,* refers to the power of the brain to create outcomes as "expectations being a function of your belief systems." He cites examples of patients with terminal pain who have dramatically changed their experience of pain by changing their perception of pain. "To a large extent, how you see your pain problem determines how you experience it."

Thomas Hanna in his book, *Somatics,* talks about the effect that your expectations can have on your health. "If we expect our bodies to be resilient and healthy, then we will remain so." Hanna goes on to give us even more responsibility for creating what happens to us: "To anticipate pathology is functionally tantamount to intending it." And in terms of our physical conditions, "If we habitually cringe in response to bodily discomforts, expecting the worst, we are chronically reinforcing this discomfort as a permanent condition which becomes resistant to improvement."

Our level of expectation affects the outcomes in every area of our lives. Expectation is the feeling of completion that guides and gives structure to performance.

The power of "expectation" can be seen in the ability of athletes who operate at this level to handle distractions. Distractions are the most common thing in the world and they corrode and destroy HiLevel Performance. Distractions take as many forms as you can imagine. Often they are attractive, as in money, someone beautiful, something that tastes or feels good. Some are deadly, as in drugs. Some are minor, like someone yelling in the crowd, or a headache. Some are major: a serious injury, or a death in the family. But it is distractions that cripple HiLevel Performance. Distractions don't care about you or your future.

If you care about yourself and what you've set out to achieve, you'll be able to identify a distraction when it happens. If you find that something seems to be disturbing your focus, simply ask yourself, "Is this something I want to do?" Your feelings, your principles, and whatever commitment you've developed will let you know. It may take a while to sort out the right answer, so take your time before responding. Distractions create people who believe they are victims.

Make it nice for yourself, learn to work hard, maintain your commitment and reach this level of confidence. Expect to do well!

## 7) Accept the Results of Your Actions.

The ability to accept the outcomes associated with your efforts involves being able to step back and be objective, to record the learning and get back to work. "Stepping back" demands the trust in yourself and in your ability to want to know how you did. "Being objective" demands the trust in yourself and in your ability to stay open to receiving feedback regarding how you did. "To record the learning" demands that you know how you did, you experience the feedback related to how you did and you record the thoughts and feelings associated with how you want to do it in the future. To truly want to accept the results of your efforts requires the strength of your commitment, the humility to recognize that you are less than perfect, and the awareness that you need feedback in order to get better.

As a HiLevel Participant, the challenge for you will be to focus on the fun and avoid comparing yourself to others.

As a HiLevel Competitor, the challenge for you will be to be nice to yourself and set realistic goals for each segment of your training.

Hard work has a way of bringing you closer to the source of your strength and this strength can help you to accept the results of your actions. For some people, this source of power is God. For others, this source takes a form that they acknowledge as a higher power. When you acknowledge the presence of God or a higher power, humility comes as you identify this source of power and the contribution it makes to your life.

Consider the relationship you have with a higher power and the meaning that this relationship has for you. In truth, physical and spiritual health can't be separated. A thriving spiritual life creates an environment for physical healing and strength. In the same way, physical well-being infuses our spirit with hope and joy. Humility is the outward expression of the respect you have for yourself, your environment and your place in it.

In studying people who were able to transform a hopeless situation into a positive situation, Csikszentmihalyi found that their strength came in the form of "un-self-conscious self-assurance." Said Csikszentmihalyi, "They did not doubt their own resources would be sufficient to allow them to determine their fate. In that sense one would call them self-assured, yet at the same time, their egos seemed curiously absent: they are not self-centered; their energy is typically not bent on dominating the environment as much as finding a way to function within it harmoniously."

To build trust on a team level, one must follow the same seven steps, but with the added responsibility of becoming a family.

1) **Set Realistic Expectations.** Team goals are made by and agreed to by all involved. Included in this agreement is an understanding of individual roles and responsibilities.

2) **Work Hard.** Individuals involved embrace what I call the Blue Collar Attitude and understand the value of pushing each other to new levels of intensity. Blue Collar in this sense means: hard work is good for you and fun.

3) **Maintain Your Fire.** Group support and trust enable the team to "get up and stay up." Each member is able to: believe in themselves, in the team and in the mission; choose to follow through to complete the mission.

4) **Stay Present.** As a whole, the group is able to: relax; rest when needed; change gears; focus on the appropriate thoughts and feelings; and maintain the interest, intensity, excitement, and passion for the mission.

5) **Stay in the Groove.** As a whole, the group is able to: maintain good form and proper technique; get into the flow; feel connected with the activity; work together and take care of business.

6) **Turn Commitment into an Expectation.** Hard work has brought the group to the place where doing well is an expectation. The circle has been tightened; feelings of cooperation, trust and love can be seen and felt.

7) **Accept the Results of Your Actions.** The group is committed to: accepting feedback and learning from their mistakes; accepting the pain and frustration associated with coming up short and playing poorly; learning how to lose; stepping back, evaluating, learning from the experience, and coming back on another day to perform well.

When you tighten the circle the team becomes a family. A relationship exists as a connection between the participating individuals. The forms and qualities of this connection are determined by the team members. As a team member, you are responsible for yourself and for the maintenance of your part of the relationship. At the level of trust, you feel good about yourself and your ability to communicate in a positive, open, and supportive manner.

To "tighten the circle" is to increase the level of communication, cooperation, trust, and love that exists between you and the people who are important to you. Psychologists tell us that individuals on a team develop trust as they are able to move through the stages of forming, norming, and storming, to performing.

**Forming.** Individuals come together, are introduced to one another and to the system. Individuals learn what is expected of them.

**Norming.** Individuals experience the system, are given a position or an assignment. Workouts and/or tryouts begin.

**Storming.** Individuals are competing to make the team or earn a starting position.

**Performing.** Individuals accept their position and their role on the team.

Team members bond as trust develops. The team works together in a cooperative fashion. Trust and love are present. The team develops the closeness of a family.

As the team reaches the level of performing and begins to operate as a family, the following characteristics are present:

**Feelings are shared.** The presence of trust and love in a group enables team members to communicate these feelings and to acknowledge individual performances and contributions. The ability to acknowledge the performance and contribution of others comes with maturity, the ability to see beyond your own needs and to recognize and have empathy for the needs of others.

Consider the words of Phil Jackson, as he talks about the importance of compassion, "love is the force that binds teams together." The love that Jackson is talking about is the ability of individuals to respect, accept, and acknowledge each other. The most efficient way to acknowledge one another is to accept teammates for who they are. Bill Curry tells his players and his coaches at the University of Kentucky, "You don't have to like one another, but I do expect you to love one another."

To "love" means to "accept." As the teacher of love, Eric Fromm once said, "Giving is the highest expression of potency."

The challenge for coaches and players who want to build the closeness of a family is to create an environment where individuals feel secure to "give" freely of their acceptance of each other. They must communicate and express acceptance, concern, empathy, approval, and love. They must be eager to make emotional deposits. Emotional deposits build a reserve of good feelings for all involved; this reserve is known as an emotional bank account.

The reserve in your emotional bank account is the trust that has been established in your relationship. This trust is what enables coaches and players to accept feedback from one another without this information taking away from the quality of the relationship. As effective leaders, both Jackson and Curry are able to express their frustration and anger with the actions of individuals and with their team, without damaging the relationship in question. In this sense they are able to be proactive. Namely, they are able to separate the person from the behavior.

You may be upset with someone and his behavior, but you accept him as a person. It may sound like a play on words; however, when you are able to separate a person from the behavior, the feelings you communicate will build rather than take away from your relationship. As emotional deposits can build trust, emotional withdrawals can destroy trust. Emotional withdrawals are negative feelings which can leave people feeling bad about themselves and their performance. An emotional withdrawal is negative verbal and nonverbal feedback, sometimes referred to as attitude, that communicates anger, judgment and lack of acceptance. Emotional withdrawals can build fear and anger. Emotional withdrawals can sabotage the chance for success and put distance between members of the group.

Emotional withdrawals can be good for you and good for your relationship. Emotional withdrawals are good for you when they: remind you of how much you care (you apologize and you work to be a better person); warn you that you are stressed (you apologize and take better care of yourself); establish your boundaries (you apologize and communicate what you want in a positive manner); get the other person's attention (you communicate your needs and the other person cooperates); bring attention to issues (you work together to build a better relationship).

The bottom line regarding your emotional bank account, as with any bank account, is your balance. When you overdraw your savings, you run the risk of losing your account and your credit. In a relationship, if you overdraw your account, you run the risk of losing the relationship and your credibility as a person who can be trusted.

In the winter of 1972, Eddie Aikau taught me a very important lesson about the value of making emotional deposits. Aikau and I were sitting in the lineup at Sunset Beach; it was right before dark on New Year's Eve. We had first met back in 1965. I had just arrived from the mainland and I was learning to surf in Hawaii. Aikau and his family, brothers Clyde and Gerald and his parents, "Mom" and "Pops" Aikau, were already established as "primary players" in the north shore surf scene. To be friends with the Aikau family was an important step for me.

As Aikau began to be recognized as a premier big wave surfer, the acclaim that he received did not change him or our relationship. When I started surfing Sunset Beach he welcomed me with open arms, he taught me how to line up the different swells and from time to time he even gave me waves. On this particular night we were surfing alone for about an hour. The swell was extremely north, which meant the waves were really long and relatively easy to make. I was surfing way over my head as we took turns taking off from as far over as possible and hooting as we made it all the way through to the inside. I remember it as one of my all-time favorite sessions.

Toward the end of the session, Aikau paddled over and grabbed the rail of my board and as we slapped hands he said, "Hey, Brad, we're Bra'da Bra'da." I said something weak like, "you bet," not really knowing the full meaning of what he meant.

That night at our customary New Year's Eve party, I checked it out with Barry Kanaiaupuni as I recounted what had happened. "Hey, Barry, what exactly did Aikau mean, 'Bra'da Bra'da'?"

Barry replied, "You know, family, feelings that are deep, feelings of cooperation, trust and love. Eddie is telling you that he is your friend and that you can count on him."

To say you could "count on Eddie" is a major understatement; Aikau was totally committed to his family and his friends. Aikau taught me that 'Bra'da Bra'da' is a special feeling, a feeling that builds:

**a)** **Family.** Aikau had the ability to tighten the circle, to bring people closer together. He made me feel special and his trust inspired me to surf hard in his presence.

**b)** **Strength.** Aikau exuded feelings of cooperation, trust and love. He was able to do this because he worked hard to develop his skills in the water; he was in great shape and his belief in himself and what he did was absolute.

c) **Cooperation.** The Quicksilver surfwear company captured Aikau's spirit in the phrase, "Eddie would go." Indeed, he would go, he would paddle out to attempt to surf the biggest surf imaginable; he would paddle out to save swimmers as part of his job as a life guard at Waimea Bay; he would paddle to get your board in the rip tide at Sunset Beach and then bring it to you. . . something he did for me on more than one occasion.

d) **Love.** Aikau had a passion for surfing big waves, saving people's lives, and being a good friend. Aikau also had a passion for learning all he could about his heritage. As part of his commitment he joined the Polynesian Voyaging Society and became part of the second crew of the Hokule'a. This particular voyage was built around the idea of demonstrating that the Polynesians were able to travel inter-island on their sailing canoes using a system of celestial navigation. The Hokule'a set sail from Honolulu Harbor in the spring of 1978 with winds estimated to 35 knots. The sailing canoe capsized in the Molakai Channel. Aikau had brought a rescue surfboard for just such an occasion and he paddled to get help. Aikau was never seen again. Aikau's actions were an expression of his loyalty and love for his fellow crew members.

# Bra'da Bra'da

Bra'da Bra'da is synonymous with deep feelings of cooperation, trust and love. In 1987, Nicki Black designed the Bra'da Bra'da logo, an important psychological reminder of the importance of trust.

'Bra'da Bra'da' is synonymous with deep feelings of cooperation, trust and love. In 1987, Nicki Black designed the Bra'da Bra'da logo, an important psychological reminder of the importance of trust.

The ability of a team to develop trust and operate as a family is also dependent on leadership. The leadership in question is a "two-way street," as coach and team members share equally in this responsibility. While the coach is responsible for establishing and maintaining the direction of the program, the team members are responsible for "buying into" the program and maintaining the support for each other and for the program. A team that is able to maintain this level of leadership is said to have "good chemistry." The essence of this chemistry is loyalty, the ability to be there for your teammates and for the team. As Brian Biro points out in *Beyond Success,* "As a leader nothing is more important than building trust. And nothing is more important to trust than being fully present for those you lead."

**Issues must be identified and resolved**. As the team begins to operate as a family, the team members are eager to meet on a regular basis to identify and resolve any and all issues that could become a distraction to the team. A format for these meetings is established that allows for feelings to be shared, compromises to be made, and a solution reached within a predetermined time frame. The focus of these meetings is to resolve the issue, for each member to take responsibility for their actions.

Joe Paterno described this level of responsibility in talking about drug education:

> *"I put it to my players straight up. I tell*
> *them I'm turning the team over to them. I*
> *will continue to be in charge, but the*
> *responsibility of policing one another is up*
> *to them. They need to be in charge of one*
> *another. If I need to step in and discipline I*
> *will, but they need to tell me this. I refuse*
> *to set up a game of rules and regulations*
> *that encourages them to beat the system.*
> *They are the system and we will be as good*
> *as they are in terms of being in charge of*
> *themselves and one another."*

**There is synergy.** When Abraham Maslow spoke of synergy, he was referring to a concept invented and developed by Ruth Benedict in 1941. Benedict was a noted anthropologist, and synergy was the term she used to compare societies as to the amount of aggression present in their social order. She concluded that a society that had a high synergy rating was one where one person's gain would result in a gain for all. Conversely, in a low synergy society, one person's gain might result in a victory over another (that is, someone loses). Therefore, the amount of synergy present is dependent upon the willingness of the members to work together.

On a team with synergy, the total effort of the team is greater than the sum of individuals' efforts. The team has come together to produce an effort that far exceeds what could be accomplished as individuals.

This sets the stage for individual and team performance levels to soar. As the team begins to operate as a family and synergy is present, its members eagerly work hard developing the collective ability to maintain the fire, stay present, stay in the groove, turn team commitment into an expectation, and accept the results of the group effort. The end result is that individuals will perform up to and beyond their potential and the team will likewise reach new levels of performance.

The following story is an excellent example of the power of synergy. This story is entitled "Lacro versus Punahou." A tiny school from rural Kauai, Waimea High School, was about to play Punahou School from Honolulu for the State Volleyball Championship. Punahou has been called "a factory for producing volleyball legends." The year was 1984. The State Volleyball Championships were being held on Kauai for the first time. Lyman Lacro played for Waimea High School and he was a junior.

Punahou was loaded with Trevor Schirman, Danny McInerny, Sio Saipiaa, Hugh Foster, and several other really good players who averaged 6'5" across the front line. Schirman, McInerny, Saipiaa, and Foster all went to Division One programs on volleyball scholarships, Schirman played on the U. S. National team, and Foster is said to have been one of the most dominant high school players ever.

Lacro and his teammates had the goal of getting into the finals, playing on Saturday in front of their hometown friends. Waimea's two best players were Lacro, 5'11", and Barry Magaoay, 5'10". Waimea ran one play, Lacro and Magaoay took turns setting each other a two and hitting into the strength of Punahou's defense. In reality, Waimea didn't have a chance. Two good players, both setters, were playing in the middle, hitting against the heart of Punahou's defense.

As Lacro describes what made this match, he begins by describing how impressed he and his teammates were with Punahou's height, tradition, and with the athletes they had. The scores of the two games were something like 15-6, 15-4 in favor of Punahou. Yet Lacro declares that this match was a huge win for his team.

The match was a win because, as Lacro explains,

> *"We made it a game, we had long rallies and we made Punahou earn their points. When we finished we were happy with our efforts; we were gratified because we felt that we had maxed our potential; we were exhausted and we knew that we had played with heart; we had done our absolute best."*

Synergy was present; everyone on the team accepted their roles and worked together despite the fact that it was largely a two-man attack. The role of Lacro and Magaoay was simple: control the ball. The roles of the other four players on the floor were: pass the ball to Lacro and Magaoay and don't hit out. The team performed beyond its ability.

The coaches that day for Punahou were Peter Balding and Chris McLachlin, who was so impressed with Lacro's performance that day that he later hired him to be the head coach of Punahou's Boys Varsity Volleyball Team. Lyman Lacro coached Punahou to the State Championships in 1994, 1995, and 1996.

## In Summary

The development of trust in yourself and your teammates can produce new levels of expectancy, expression, health and well-being, cooperation, effectiveness, teamwork, synergy, performance, and fun. Trust in yourself or your teammates is like peak physical conditioning—hard to build and easy to lose. Injuries, sickness, a poor performance, inconsistent behavior or a heartbreaking loss can leave you and your teammates feeling emotionally bankrupt. Trust, as a step to PrimeTime, requires total dedication to reach and experience to maintain. In order to continue on with the process, stay true to your mission, live your truth and "expect it to happen."

The following terms emphasize important principles in the process of creating trust.

## As an individual:

**Reality.** Set goals that are within your reach.

**Blue Collar.** Enjoy the hard work; PrimeTime and hard work go hand in hand.

**Mission.** Establish your direction and stay on track.

**Focus.** Affirm your ability to feel confident, to be physically and emotionally up for the challenge, and to follow through with right choices.

**Take Care of Business.** Train yourself to maintain your interest, intensity, excitement and passion for your performance.

**Flow.** Learn to lose yourself in the action, to become one with the work and fun that got you there.

**Expect.** Work hard to get to a place where you just know it will happen. Keep pushing.

**Learn.** Embrace the learning and apply the lessons; the road to PrimeTime is never smooth or easy.

## As a team:

**Bra'da Bra'da.** Share the love and pull everyone in.

**Loyalty.** Be there for one another and let your actions reflect this commitment.

**Clarity.** Keep the mission of the team in view at all times; distractions are a waste of time and energy.

**Efficient.** Work together and share in the gains.

**PrimeTime.** Experience the happiness and rewards, results well worth the work.

## PrimeTime Wrap

Consider the case of Bruce Eliashof, M.D., age 30, HiLevel Board Member and Chief Resident of the Psychiatric Resident Program of San Mateo General Hospital in San Mateo. Eliashof, born and raised in Hawaii, is an accomplished surfer, windsurfer, paddler, and snowboarder.

He is a serious competitor. He could use medical school as an excuse to play it safe. He doesn't. He sails and surfs harder than ever: forward and backward loops, speed runs, aerials, floaters, turns off the lip and coming from behind huge barrels. He has all of the moves to compete at any level in both sports.

Eliashof could use the cold water of California as an excuse to get comfortable. He doesn't. He made the adjustment to sailing and surfing in a full wet suit in water that ranges from 48 to 60 degrees and air temperatures as low as 50 degrees. You have to want it really bad to confront the elements and win. Imagine performing the most difficult maneuver in your activity with your feet numb.

Speaking of Eliashof, Bernie Baker observed, "To tackle both extremes, the tropical conditions in Hawaii and the nail biting cold of Northern California and be successful requires a very special person. Eliashof is one of those people who would stand out on this planet no matter what he did!"

He does not use his busy medical schedule as an excuse to slow down, either. He works fifty-hour weeks and sails and surfs five to six times per week. Imagine working an eight-hour day in San Mateo, driving an hour-and-a-half to Santa Cruz, and still having enough energy to compete with local pros who windsurf for a living.

Eliashof has passion for his sports and their blue collar work habits. He works very hard at getting better at the sports he loves. He explains,

> *"I feel very lucky, I love my work and I love to compete at HiLevel. I will continue to push myself to get better and to take the risks that make sense to me. I lead my life full out for a reason. I love the feeling that comes with knowing I can trust my ability and myself to pull off radical moves in extreme conditions. I thrive on knowing I can work hard and play hard. I always want to be able to show up and give my best effort in the sports I love. That's what being a HiLevel competitor means to me."*

In step six, you learned how to build trust. In step seven, you will learn how to experience growth. Colonel Pat Mente once said, "Keep fighting; you never know when you are winning."

In the field of exercise physiology, the term "summation of the forces," describes the cooperation that goes on in the body when all of your muscles are working together in harmony. For example, the stroke in paddling a canoe or kayak involves the push of the legs, the contraction of the abdominal muscles, and the pull of the upper body. The push of the legs provides the leverage, the contraction of the abdominal muscles provides support for the lower back and the pull of the upper body propels you forward. The cooperation between your lower body, your abdominal muscles and your upper body allows you to be more efficient, to avoid injury and to increase the power of your stroke.

# STEP SEVEN
# Work what you've learned.

In personal growth, there is a cooperation that goes on between your mind, body, and spirit. The mind provides the push, the leverage from working the previous six steps, the body provides the support, the physical strength and emotional intensity to perform within a safe range, and the spirit provides the pull, the will to get better and complete the growth process. Growth can be viewed in many ways.

## Growth as an Experience.

Growth is the process of learning a new behavior. If this new behavior becomes part of you, then you have experienced growth and your behavior reflects this growth. For example, you decide to participate in a growth-related camp, complete with a high ropes course. As you return to your regular activities, your friends notice you are different. If this "different" behavior wears off after a few weeks, your new behavior was merely a change in your personality. However, if your new behavior becomes part of you, then you experienced growth and your behavior reflects this growth.

*Growth and Your Performance.* In terms of your performance, growth is the ability to capitalize on the trust you have built in yourself and learn new skills that represent a reach for you physically and emotionally; increase the intensity of your workouts and performances; take

# Growth Laminates

Growth creates a lamination effect. After every learning cycle with mind, body, and spirit cooperating at new levels, new layers of efficiency, strength, and incentive are deposited.

You feel the powerful push of your confidence, the leverage of your absolute belief and trust in yourself and in your ability. You are calm and relaxed under pressure, all of your energy is applied to your performance. You know that you can take a risk and learn and grow from your experience. You believe in your ability to create PrimeTime.

You feel the support of your fitness, the physical strength and endurance of your body and the emotional control of your intensity. You are able to focus on your feelings in extreme situations. You quickly recognize the signals related to fatigue, overuse and/or injury.

You feel the pull of your commitment; you are eager to complete your mission. Your ability to accept the results of your efforts, to seek feedback and apply the learning to your performance makes you eager to take on new challenges. You want to be the best that you can be. You want to experience the joy that comes when your beliefs, feelings and choices about what you want to do operate in harmony.

the risks associated with your new level of participation; actively seek the feedback related to your performance, apply this learning and practice letting go of negative thoughts and feelings.

## Growth and the Challenge.

The challenge is to be objective as you evaluate your situation and performance level. As Annabella Hofmann points out: "see things as they are and not as you have created them in your mind." Change ineffective behavior: thoughts, feelings or actions that do not work for you. To resist the temptation to play it safe and repeat a familiar pattern, get out of your mind and focus on your feelings related to learning a new way of doing things. Let go of negative experiences. Process your pain, fear and/or anger mentally, physically, emotionally and spiritually. Get out of the victim mode and get into the solution mode. Embrace the learning that a negative experience has to offer; stay out of the "suck" and turn your experience into a "swell." Failure, as Deepak Chopra suggests, is actually a "seed for success." From your failures you learn the lessons that allow you to be who you really want to become and to learn to do things the way you really want to do them.

## Growth as Hard Work.

Growth, by definition is hard work. Growth involves hours of practice and the discipline to follow a rigorous training program. It means getting better, bigger, and stronger. It involves taking risks, stepping beyond your comfort zone and learning new skills. Eagerness to work hard, hunger, perhaps even aggression may be part of it. Kenny Miller, the former Olympic Marathon runner described the growth required to compete at the Olympic level: "You must channel a ferocious spirit into a spirit of competition." The push to work this hard comes from your mind as you condition yourself to believe in yourself, to have the "yes, I can" attitude.

## Growth as a Process.

The growth process begins with an idea that you want to accomplish something that represents a test, a push and a challenge for you mentally, physically, and spiritually. To check your readiness for this challenge, make sure three things are in order. Be confident in your ability to handle the inherent risk. Be able to focus physically and emotionally at this level. Be eager to complete the experience. Completion of the growth experience will require cooperation among your mind, body, and spirit. If you are to step outside of your comfort zone and perform at your very best, the idea of what you want to accomplish must be accompanied by an attitude, belief, thought, feeling, decision, and choice that support your ability to perform at this level. Only then can you complete the growth process.

## Growth and Your Mind.

Growth as it relates to your mind is the attitude and the belief that, as Colonel Mente points out, you can keep going and you can expect the best. You have the mental toughness to remain positive and open and to believe in yourself in the most difficult of situations. You know you can learn new skills, increase your intensity level, take a risk, and accept the results of your actions.

## Growth as an Attitude.

The growth attitude is positive and open, that is, you know you can learn and grow from this challenge. "Life is a gift of nature; a beautiful life is a gift of wisdom." said Ramtha. The attitude which supports growth is one which allows you to remain positive and open to the lessons inherent in the growth process. Wisdom is the key to a beautiful life. Working backwards, wisdom is the product of learning, and learning in terms of growth comes with risk. A positive and open attitude allows you to find the lesson in the risk and continue on with the learning process. A positive attitude towards growth is best summed up in Churchill's famous comment, "never, never, never, never give up."

Growth as an attitude represents you at your very best. Your positive attitude colors your perception, you view the events in your life, as the saying goes, "as a glass that is half-full rather than half-empty."

Growth as an attitude says that what you are doing right now is important, what you are doing right now is fun and/or worth the effort and that there will be value in the lessons learned from your experience.

Growth as an attitude allows you to create what Maxwell Maltz refers to as a "success-type personality," meaning that you have conditioned your brain to "remember past successes and forget failures." Remembering your successes allows you to program your mind for success, and forgetting your failures allows you to learn from these experiences but not to dwell on them.

Growth as an attitude allows you to experience growth in the best possible way. With your focus on the positive aspects of your experience, you condition yourself to focus on the positive and to make the most of any experience.

## Growth as a Belief.

The growth belief is confidence in your ability, that is, "I can handle this challenge." Dr. Elliot Eisner once said, "Brains are biological, minds are grown." As Dr. Eisner points out, a brain becomes a mind as a result of growth. Growth, in the form of your experiences, develops your mind, and your mind in turn provides the confidence required to put yourself in a position to experience growth.

Train your mind to identify what is important to you so that you can make growth-related decisions that are in line with your intent. Growth-related decisions involve risk, emotional and physical pain, injury, embarrassment, etc. You can learn to identify the potential risk and decide if the risk in question is worth it. You can also evaluate the cost of the risk after your performance and record the learning and decide what you would have done differently.

Belief in yourself and your abilities allows you to decide to operate outside your comfort zone and be comfortable with your decision. Claudia Manno, 28, a serious windsurfer who talks about her desire to windsurf at Back Yards, said to me, "Last year I sailed at Back Yards with its big waves. It is scary. . . [pause], but I love the challenge."

Manno accepts her fear as part of the learning process. Growth and risk go hand in hand. Your capacity to "learn, feel, change, grow, love or live," is dependent on your ability to take risks. Closely related to your ability to take risks is your ability to learn from experience. To take a risk is meaningless by itself; to take a risk and learn from your efforts is the foundation of growth. To take a risk and experience growth is to identify the lesson and record the learning.

Growth as a belief can become a way of life, characterized by your looking for opportunities to develop skills, to become better at what you do, to experience the joy that comes with becoming all that you can become. Citing Ram Dass, "You just start from where you are, not where you wish you were, and your givens are certain trainings and skills and responsibilities— then the game is to find within . . . how to use it all as a method of working on yourself." Ram Dass is describing the belief that growth is the product of applying yourself fully to the activities that make up your life.

## Growth and Your Body.

You have the fire and the focus to keep going. Growth as it relates to your body is the physical and emotional conditioning to create the feelings needed to keep going, to take care of business. You have clarity to think about what you want to have happen and the strength and the endurance to perform at this level. Your ability to focus allows you to generate the intensity you need to be up for the challenge.

## Growth as a Thought.

The growth thought is clear and exact, such as, "I know what I want to accomplish!" I am reminded of the vision of Norman Cousins: "The capacity to envision life as it could be, to think in new dimensions, and to be aware of new possibilities." The thoughts about what you want to achieve give you direction. The thoughts about what you want to achieve are both narrow and broad: narrow, in that they represent a clear picture of what you want to accomplish, and broad in that they represent all of the options open to you. As Cousins pointed out, people who are oriented towards growth are able "to envision life as it could be," and to "think in new dimensions and to be aware of new possibilities."

Thoughts which support growth are ones that provide clear vision of what you want and, at the same time, provide a framework for accepting the result of your efforts. To experience growth is to realize that the result of your efforts is always an opportunity to learn important lessons. The idea that there is perfection in the universe is centered around the idea that life will present you with lessons until the lesson which is critical for your success is learned.

Growth as a thought and growth as a belief are closely related. Wayne Dyer talks about your determination to succeed as "nothing more than your thought to do so." The belief in yourself as a successful person based on your experience is what allows you to have thoughts about yourself being successful. Dyer goes on to describe the power of your thoughts to create success in your life. "It is not what is in the world that determines the quality of your life, it is how you choose to process your world in your thoughts."

Growth as a thought speaks to the power of visualization. You need to picture yourself in your mind doing, being, and having the experiences that will result in your actively creating PrimeTime. Remember Maltz: "Mental pictures offer us an opportunity to 'practice' new traits and attitudes, which otherwise we could not do. This is possible because your nervous system cannot tell the difference between an actual experience and one that is vividly imagined."

Growth as a thought speaks to the need to practice having what I like to call "clean thoughts." Clean means that your thoughts accurately represent you at your very best. Clean thoughts are not contaminated by fear, anger, or a false sense of reality. They represent the purity of your passion for creating your version of PrimeTime.

## Growth as a Feeling.

The growth feeling is strong and steady: I am physically and emotionally ready to perform at this level. Max Lerner speaks of a "core of strength within you that survives all hurt." He argues that the turning point in your life is discovering this. This core of strength is the courage to take a risk, to put your best effort on the line and then handle a defeat or a poor effort. The courage to handle a setback is also what will allow you to seek feedback, to adapt, and to make changes.

The source of your strength and courage has to do with the interest to maintain your attention (the desire to learn from your efforts), the intensity to maintain your focus (the desire to increase your performance level), the excitement to maintain your physical and emotional presence (to welcome the pain and discomfort of performing at this level and monitor your feelings), and the passion to maintain your intention (the eagerness to express your fire).

The feelings that come up for you as you step outside your comfort zone are a source of support. They can be a reminder of how hard you need to work and/or how much you need to rest. They can be an indication of how important what you are doing is to you. They can also be a source of motivation, a signal to work harder or a red flag, a warning to slow down and take better care of yourself.

You must learn to balance your discipline and sensitivity. Discipline is associated with the desire to work hard, to be in control, and to work in a linear, step-by-step manner. Sensitivity is associated with the desire to listen to your instincts, to your intuitions, to be creative and follow your heart. Both discipline and sensitivity are important. Discipline allows you to get the job done, and sensitivity allows you to express your feelings about what is important to you. Discipline and sensitivity need to be balanced. Too much discipline and you eliminate the fun. Too much sensitivity and you don't get the job done.

I recall flying to the Big Island of Hawaii to make a presentation to the Hawaii Tennis Professionals. My health was not good and I had some anxiety about my performance. As I began my talk, I was amazed at how good I felt. Everything went well up to the halfway point. As we took a break, one of the officials came over and requested that I present some information on relaxation during the second half. I hadn't planned to present this information, but I agreed to follow his suggestion. As I started the second half of my presentation, I left my prepared outline. Suddenly it occurred to me that my audience was not with me. Try as I might, I couldn't get them back. The harder I tried, the more anxious I became and the worse I felt about my performance. I ended my talk early and could feel the anxiety starting to build. For a few days I agonized over my presentation. Out of my pain came the realization of how much I wanted to learn to be flexible on my feet during a presentation.

In review of the presentation in question, I saw that my discipline kept me committed to presenting the information on relaxation—racing, in fact, to get finished. My sensitivity was signaling me to slow down and change gears and I didn't know how. The pain I felt was evidence of how much I wanted to learn to be a good speaker. My sensitivity supported me in finding out what was important to me and in learning to be more creative during a presentation.

Feelings are crucial to the growth process; be sensitive to your feelings and listen to the signals that your body is sending you. There is a difference between the feelings associated with healthy growth and those associated with muscle tears and strains. The red flags in this area are recurring injuries and chronic fatigue. These are warning signs that you are training too hard and you need a rest. Listening to the signals that your body is sending will allow you to balance how hard you work, play, rest, and relax. Taking care of yourself is essential to growth. Just as rest is important to the body builder who is training for growth, taking care of yourself insures that you will be ready to give your best effort.

Red flags or warning signs that you have taken too big a risk or stepped too far outside your comfort zone come up when you begin to have serious doubts and negative thoughts and feelings about your ability. In situations like these, you need to ask yourself why you are afraid and what you really want to have happen.

Growth as a feeling speaks to the link between your thoughts and your feelings. Psychologists have pointed out that it is impossible to have a thought without a feeling or conversely to have a feeling without a thought. The key is to choose your thoughts carefully—thoughts which represent you well. Monitor your feelings carefully, as they provide the awareness you need to stay on track. Growth as a feeling relates to the strength of your interest, intensity, excitement, and passion for doing what you love.

## Growth and Your Spirit.

Growth, as it relates to your spirit is the ability to make a decision based on what you want to have happen, (you know where you are going and follow through with the right choices; you know why you want to do this). The relationship between the intellectual act of making a decision and the physical act of carrying out a choice involves a delicate balance of clarity and intensity.

Clarity is to make the decision appropriate for you, the one that has just the right amount of risk, readily apparent. The decision you make about what you want to accomplish becomes your intention.

Intensity is the physical and emotional strength and endurance to choose each moment to carry out your decision. The choice to carry out your decision becomes your attention.

The concept of "walking your talk" applies here. You want your intention—what you say you are going to do—to match up with your attention or what you do. "Walking your talk," whether you verbalize your decision or keep it to yourself, has to do with making good on your word. Given the implied risk in growth decisions, your ability to make good on your word will impact your future growth in the following ways: mentally, you will have confidence in your ability to make growth decisions (keeping your word to yourself builds your self-esteem); physically, you will be more inclined to express your fire (you know you can get intense and stay intense); spiritually, you will have faith in your ability to follow through (to choose to be intense). As Robert Nideffer points out, "Making a choice and having faith in that choice helps quiet the voice of doubt and conflict in your mind."

## Growth as a Decision.

The growth decision is set (I have reviewed my options, I know what is expected and I am going for it!). Growth as a decision has to do with the eagerness to show up ready, give your best effort, and accept the results of your efforts. Acceptance, in this regard, is a quiet reflection of the way things are, like Reinhold Niebuhr's serenity prayer: "God grant me the serenity to accept the things I cannot change, the courage to change the things I can and the wisdom to know the difference."

Serenity is the strength to accept, to let go of negative, self-defeating thoughts and feelings related to performance. Courage, in the form of your commitment, allows you to evaluate your performance, to learn the inherent lessons and then get back to work. Wisdom, in the form of your experience, allows you to focus on the portions of your performance you can control: your best effort, your best performance on a given occasion.

Andrew Weil, a medical doctor with a Harvard education, describes the act of acceptance. After he graduated from Harvard, Weil was disenchanted with the medical approach to healing. He spent the next few years searching in Colombia, Ecuador, and Peru for shamans who could teach him secrets of healing patients. After years of frustration, Weil decided that he had been looking in the wrong place. He concluded that the secret to healing patients existed inside each person. Weil explained, "I did not have to turn from my own land and culture, my formal education, and my own self to find the source of healing. But I did need to spend those years wandering in order to figure that out." Weil had the maturity to accept the result of his efforts.

## Growth as Feedback.

In order to experience growth you need feedback. You need to accept the reality of your situation. In my work with athletes, I have been amazed at how hard it is for some people to accept the reality of their situations. At the end of the semester in my Sports Psychology class, I ask my students to evaluate their mental toughness, ability to focus and ability to maintain their commitment. Then I sit down individually with each student and we discuss the evaluation.

I came away from two such interviews feeling really good about the progress of two students. One was a young man who played point guard on the basketball team, and the other was a young woman who was a striker on the soccer team. Both athletes felt they were mentally tough and capable of focusing completely. Shortly after our interviews, I ran into their respective coaches. Both coaches knew that these athletes were enrolled in my course and both of them wanted to know about their progress. In both cases, I replied in a positive manner, stating how happy I was with their progress. I was shocked when both coaches presented a completely different point of view about these two athletes.

The coaches felt that both athletes were selfish, lacking mental toughness, extremely temperamental and, at times, very lazy. How could the opinion these athletes had of themselves be so different from the opinion of their coaches? To find out the answer, I consulted with Dr. René Tillich, who observed, "The higher the pathology, the greater the distortion in reality." In other words, the more damage experienced in childhood, the more damage to the psyche (pathology) and the greater the distortion in reality.

The answer to my question was simple: both of these young people were unable to accept the reality of their situations. They were unable to accept feedback which was inconsistent with the image they had of themselves. The answer for these two young athletes and for you, if you have difficulty accepting feedback, is to work on your self-esteem: train your mind to accept both positive and negative feedback, learn from this feedback, and express this learning in your performance. Feedback regarding your performance comes from your body, feelings, and actions.

The feedback from your body comes in the form of muscle tension, fatigue level, and overall well-being. Performances which go well tend to leave you feeling relaxed, energized, and good about yourself. Performances which go poorly leave you feeling tense, drained, and not so good about yourself. For example, I think of my colleague Dan Morrison, Head Football Coach and Dean at Punahou School. As a young coach, Dan was attached to a belief that he was being judged by the success of his team and the belief that to settle for anything less than perfection from himself and others meant he didn't care. When Dan's team did not play well, his body became tense, especially his hands, shoulders, and neck.

The feedback from your feelings comes as you become aware of what your emotions mean to you. In Dan's case, when his team did not play well, he felt angry at his players.

The feedback from your actions usually comes from your coaches, teammates, players, friends, and family. Again in Dan's case, his players responded to his anger by becoming confused and frustrated, and by breaking eye contact and looking away during time-outs.

As Morrison became aware of the feedback from his body, feelings, and actions, he developed the following strategy: To process his tension he learned to stop what he was doing, put his hands on his knees, take a deep breath and put his focus on his players. To process his feelings of anger and frustration he let go of the belief that his players' performance had to do with him. To learn and grow from his experience he changed his focus from himself to his players. He trained himself to listen to his players, to reflect his hurt back as love and concern for them. The irony is that as his focus changed, as he learned to accept the feedback from his body, his feelings, and his actions, his team began to play better.

## Growth as a Choice.

Growth as a choice will complete the process: I will carry out the plan; I will maintain my physical and emotional intensity; I will record the learning and I will let go of any negative emotions.

Growth as a choice involves intensity. The act of being intense is when it all comes together: the harmony between your beliefs, feelings, and choices. You have decided to give 100% of your effort, to go all out, to attend fully to what you are doing. To accomplish this level of participation, you will need to choose each moment to be intense based on your belief that you can and the feeling that you are excited to express your fire.

To maintain this level of intensity is intoxicating: the emotional and physical feelings associated with this state are what are often referred to as the "zone" or "flow" state. Biondi refers to this state as "the pure joy associated with doing what I love." Bradshaw refers to this state as "the feeling that goes with working so hard that I bring myself present and everything else around me washes away." Goleman defines this state:

> *"Flow is a state devoid of emotional static, save for a compelling, highly motivating feeling of mild ecstasy. That ecstasy seems to be a byproduct of the attentional focus that is a prerequisite of flow. Indeed, the classic literature of contemplative traditions describes states of absorption that are experienced as pure bliss; flow induced by nothing more than intense concentration."*

Growth as a choice involves recording the learning. Psychologists talk about the importance of self-esteem as it relates to learning and the "moment of choosing," the time of reflection between your thought and the action that follows. The role that self-esteem plays in this process has to do with your ability to review your decision and make the right choice. If you feel good about yourself you will have the confidence to review your decision and the right choice will be readily apparent. Conversely, if you don't feel good about yourself, you will not have the confidence to review your decision and you will have difficulty seeing and recognizing the right choice.

Growth as a choice involves learning to let go. The growth choice will complete the process: I will carry out the plan, record the learning, and let go of any negative emotions. Letting go is a skill that begins in the body and ends in the mind. Letting go follows Maltz's guidelines for forgetting your failures. Once you have learned from your experience, you need to let the negative emotions go. You decide that you are willing to give up a negative thought or feeling and then choose a technique that enables you to release these emotions. As you breathe deeply, your breathing signals the body to relax, and as you let these feelings go, your body feels the release of these emotions.

The "growth choice" is the choice that allows you to take a risk and learn and grow from your efforts. As Sheldon Kopp says, "You must learn to make the growth choice, not the fear choice." The "fear choice" is the choice that allows you to play it safe, to repeat an unwanted pattern of behavior. The "growth choice" means that you embrace the opportunity to process these emotions. The "fear choice" would be to back away from these emotions, denying their existence and relevance to you. The choice to learn from your emotions involves the maturity to be aware of your feelings, to confront them and let the negative feelings go.

Phil Jackson describes the importance of letting go in this way.

> *"I used to believe that the day I could accept defeat was the day I would have to give up my job. But losing is an integral part of the dance of winning. Buddhism teaches us that by accepting death, you discover life. Similarly, only by acknowledging the possibility of defeat can you fully experience the joy of competition. Our culture would have us believe that being able to accept loss is tantamount to setting yourself up to lose. But not everyone can win all the time; obsessing adds an unnecessary layer of pressure that constricts body and spirit and, ultimately, robs you of the freedom to do your best."*

I suggest a computer analogy to help complete the definition of letting go. Every time you have a negative experience, the negative emotions related to this experience open a file on your hard drive (subconscious). Let's say you are playing on a team and you don't like your coach. The first time you get mad at your coach, your computer (sub-conscious) opens a file called "MAD@COACH." From that moment forward every time you get mad at your coach, the negative emotions related to this incident are stored in the file, MAD@COACH. When the file becomes full, the toxic emotions spill out and are expressed outwardly as an angry rage or tantrum, or inwardly as depression or a physical illness or both. Letting go is a way of processing the emotions—deleting the file—and preventing a toxic buildup of negative emotions. I like the view in Deepak Chopra's *The Path of Love* which says that negative feelings about the past hold you hostage, and the key to your freedom lies in your ability to let go.

Letting go occurs on all levels: spiritual, physical, mental, and emotional. Spiritually, you must be willing to confront your pain, anger and frustration. In extreme situations, given the intensity of the emotions, letting go may need to be postponed until the experience settles. In this case, the emotions will need to be put on the back burner, and the desire to let go at some point will have to be good enough.

I remember just such an occasion involving Robby Naish. I was sitting with two young friends at Diamond Head. Robby was sailing against Josh Stone in the wave event of the OP World Cup, 1991. Josh Stone was declared the winner. A shock wave went through the entire windsurfing world. A brash young challenger had beaten the champion. In my mind, Naish was clearly the winner. Naish was livid, a huge argument broke out between Naish and the judges, a protest was filed and yet the verdict was final and Naish was upset. Naish felt cheated, angry and extremely upset at what he considered a complete injustice.

To deal with his upset, he immediately began to sail one of his three rigs back to a spot about four hundred yards down the beach. As he returned one rig, he then ran back up the beach past where I was sitting with my young friends, picked up another rig and sailed it back. Each time Naish ran by, I was amazed at the intensity of his stride, the strength of his body and the commitment that spoke out loudly and clearly as he completed this simple task. As I turned to comment to my friends, I could see that they were unable to comprehend Naish and his level of intensity, an intensity that has become as much of a trademark as his pink sails. Naish was clearly upset and his way of handling his upset was to express himself physically, to run hard and sail hard.

Letting go of negative emotions begins with the decision to confront the issue and ends in a particular style. For Naish in the above example,

# Letting Go

Kahea Hart speaks about letting go of anger.

*"Well, last season I broke twelve boards in some pretty intense wipeouts. So I was upset and angry a lot. I would get angry and then depressed because my equipment wasn't working in critical situations. I knew I would be surfing better if my boards were working. To handle my upset I've developed a strategy for letting go of my anger. First I go into my room, relax, and focus on my breathing and listen to music. Then I go outside and lift weights and work on my punching bag. The combination of relaxation and exercise allows me to process my anger. Then I focus on the solution to my problem."*

**Physically**, letting go involves breathing, relaxation, and exercise. Exercise provides a psychological release for the stress related to negative emotions and experiences. Since stress is cumulative, letting go takes on a new meaning for you if you are attempting to maintain peak conditioning. Given the harmful relationship between toxic stress and your immune system, you would be well advised to practice letting go on a regular basis.

**Mentally**, letting go involves reframing your experience and/or putting your negative emotions on the back burner. Be careful not to let negative emotions linger on the back burner or they are liable to become toxic. You need to reframe them, process them, and get rid of them.

**Emotionally**, letting go is doing what Chopra refers to as "inner work." Inner work can mean prayer, meditation, and/or writing and talking about your upset. The idea is to embrace your emotions, learn from them, and let them go.

he first had to work his way physically through the upset before he could process the frustration and anger he felt that day. The challenge for you will be to find the style that best suits your personality.

As you learn to express your own style of letting go, the crucial question is: Do you recognize your red flags? Warning signs include tantrums, basic resistance, reliving the past, or reframing the exercise without effect.

Tantrums are reverting back to childlike ways of expressing anger. They are a clear sign that childhood issues are at work. Basic resistance is a defense mechanism that signals a history of not wanting to deal with the issue in question. Again, Chopra: "Resistance is actually born of fear, and fear comes from having been deeply hurt in the past." Reliving the past is an issue that represents avoided or repressed emotions. Chopra: "There is a law of the unconscious that whatever you avoid will come back, and the more you avoid it, the stronger it will return." The Reframing exercise is not always effective. When it doesn't work or help, it is apparent that your anger runs very deep and it may be complicated by your simply not knowing how to lose.

One thorny issue, in fact, that most athletes face at some point is the difficulty of losing. You may have an inability to lose without deep personal damage. As Muhammad Ali said, "No one knows what to say in the loser's locker room." Anyone who has been involved in sports knows how painful it is to put your best effort on the line and come up short. However, the pain is a reminder of how much you care and if you truly want to get better you will need to learn "how to lose," not learn to lose. Learning how to lose means you can step back, learn from your experience and incorporate the lessons. Albert Einstein said it best when he said, "Try not to become a man of success but rather try to become a man of value." The value to be stressed in terms of losing is patience: the patience to stay true to your mission, the patience to incorporate the lessons, and the patience to come back on another day and give your best effort.

There are, to be sure, pitfalls to growth as a choice. In my work with student-athletes, I have found that most of these young people want to experience growth. Most of these young people want to: step up from being a participant to being a competitor, move up to the next level of competition; increase their performance in the classroom and on the athletic field, get better grades, get bigger, stronger, and faster; and be more intense, increase their ability to focus mentally, physically, and spiritually.

Unfortunately, some of these young people fall into one of three categories and as a result fall way short of their stated goals and expectations. The three categories are as follows:

"Stay, Go, Stay" types fail to experience the growth that they want to because they are unable to make a decision. They say they want to get more intense in their performance and yet their efforts in this regard are inconsistent. "Stay, Go, Stay" describes their approach to getting intense: on some days they are, and on some days they are not.

The coaching point here is two-part. Make sure you are clear that more intense is what you want to be; perhaps you need more information about how to get intense. Give yourself a trial period of one week. Practice being intense for a week and evaluate the results.

"Party Hardy" types fail to experience the growth because they are leading two different lives. In one of their lives they are serious and totally committed, and in their other life having fun and feeling good is their priority. Most people are unable to manage the energy requirements of these two lives. Soon the fun begins to take its toll.

The coaching point here is to be honest with yourself, to examine the results of your efforts. Do you really want to get more intense? Are you really having that much fun?

"Nobody's Home" types fail to experience the growth because they are operating in denial. They say they want to be more intense, but they haven't made a decision in this regard. Their performance and intensity levels remain unchanged. Outwardly they appear to be disconnected from their bodies; they suffer from a complete lack of focus.

The coaching point here is to build some awareness as to what you are feeling. The questions to ask are: What do you really want to do? Are you having fun?

## Summary

Growth gives meaning to your life and life to your meaning. The payoff for experiencing growth is that you feel energized, you feel a new sense of interest, intensity, excitement, and passion for what you want to accomplish. If you have clarity about this, take advantage and "Go for it!" If you don't have clarity, acknowledge that you don't and go slowly, proceed with caution.

Growth is a way of life. To make growth your focus in every area of your life, to want to learn and grow from every experience, to make the best of every situation, requires a commitment to living life to its fullest.

To want to be the best that you can be, to want to actualize all of your God-given talent, is to make growth your intention for every moment.

Growth is hard work. The gift of growth, all of the good stuff that comes with learning how to get better, is always wrapped in hard work. Without hard work, you wouldn't record the learning, as in the saying, "easy come, easy go." Without hard work you wouldn't express the learning in your performance, and growth would not happen.

Growth involves the courage to put your best effort on the line, knowing that your confidence could take a beating, your body could suffer an injury, or your spirit could be shaken.

Growth provides you with an awareness of just how important your attitude is to your well-being. Your attitude colors your belief, gives direction to your thoughts, stimulates your feelings, and shapes the decisions and choices you make.

Growth provides you with an awareness of just how important your thoughts are to your body's ability to perform, and, conversely, how important your fitness level is to your clarity and the quality of your thoughts.

Growth brings you closer to your feelings. Operating on the edge of your mental, physical, and spiritual energy levels puts you in constant contact with your feelings. These feelings are a source of support; they tell you when to pick it up and when to pack it in.

Growth is a choice. Growth requires a commitment to put your best effort on the line, over and over again. It also requires a commitment to get intense.

Growth provides you with an awareness of just how powerful you are. You have the ability to make decisions which determine the quality of your life. The choices you make from moment to moment give you control over your experience.

Growth teaches you to create PrimeTime. As you continue to learn how to let go, you will learn the lessons needed to create those moments that mean the most to you.

Growth provides you with the awareness of the importance of "keeping it light" and not taking yourself too seriously. Growth has a way of giving you a sense of humility, of giving you empathy for yourself and others. Growth has a way of teaching you about the value of humor and laughter.

The following key words emphasize the important principles of experiencing growth.

**Efficient.** The effect of being relaxed and focused in your approach.

**Strong.** The need to feel in control of your efforts.

**Experience.** The learning that comes as a result of your efforts.

**Balance.** The need to take care of business in all areas of your life.

**Fun.** The need to celebrate your efforts and enjoy the process.

**Can.** The knowledge that you have what it takes to get the job done.

**Direction.** The focus of your efforts toward your goal.

**Fire.** The strength of your passion and the will to complete the HiLevel process.

**Faith.** The trust you have in yourself to manifest your dream.

**Action.** The road to success: "doing" your best.

**Feedback.** The information you need to get better.

**Serenity.** The strength to accept/let go of emotions which do not serve you.

**Resilient.** The need to go with the flow, be flexible, swim with the current.

**Purpose.** The bottom line, what you want to have happen.

**Y**ou have arrived. You have fulfilled your dream. You have learned to express your fire. In step seven, you learned how to experience growth. In step eight, you will learn how to create PrimeTime which, by definition, is the culmination of all your efforts to express your fire and experience those special moments associated with doing what you love. To create PrimeTime is to experience the zone, to be fully in the flow. When you create PrimeTime you have learned to give your best effort and create inner harmony.

In the words of Mihaly Csikszentmihalyi,

# STEP EIGHT

# Enjoy performance with gratitude and excitement

*"When an important goal is pursued with resolution, and all one's varied activities fit together into a unified flow experience, the result is that harmony is brought to consciousness. Someone who knows his desires and works hard to achieve them is a person whose feelings, thoughts and actions are congruent with one another, and is therefore a person who has achieved inner harmony."*

In athletics we like to talk about the concept of carry-over value: what will you learn from your athletic experience that will translate into your every day life? The "harmony" that Csikszentmihalyi describes comes with learning that to give your best effort is the greatest asset you can have. To create PrimeTime is to experience what it takes to manifest those special feelings related to what you love to do. This experience and the skills you learn can be used to create PrimeTime in every area of your life.

The creation of PrimeTime can be broken down into the experience of PrimeTime and the satisfaction of creating PrimeTime. The experience of PrimeTime is made up of the feelings that go with doing what you love to do and the satisfaction has to do with knowing that you did it. The experience takes place in the present and the satisfaction comes as a reflection. The experience of PrimeTime has to do with the ability to maintain the state of being grateful, excited, and committed, and the satisfaction has to do with your ability to reach a sense of completion.

# The Catbird Seat

When you experience PrimeTime you have come full circle in the HiLevel process:

- Your energy is completely focused on what you love to do.
- Your desire has brought you to a place where you have been able to blend your creativity with your reality; your dream has come true.
- Your clarity has brought you to a place where you are able to express who you really are, and you feel good about it.
- Your interest has allowed you to learn from your efforts.
- Your intensity has allowed you to focus on getting better.
- Your excitement has kept you physically and emotionally involved.
- Your passion has enabled you to express your fire.
- Your expectation has brought you to a place where you can live your own truth.

The experience of PrimeTime involves learning to apply the universal principle of "love what you do and do what you love." As Chopra says, "Love is a state of being. It is the state in which you are in contact with being." The process of following the steps to this level of performance will require everything you have to give and give you back a new sense of yourself. When you are able to express your love, as Chopra points out, you are in a state that reflects the love that is you.

Indeed, experiencing PrimeTime is a wonderful place to be! You have learned to "light a fire" as big and as bright as you are! You have worked hard to get here and the work has given you back the ability to create joy, love, and serenity. You have the ability to maintain the state of being grateful, excited, and committed.

**Grateful** As you contemplate moments of PrimeTime, you are grateful. Grateful, in HiLevel terms, is the end product of confidence. Grateful is the state of psychological readiness, a place where you are looking forward to the most important moments of your competition or performance.

I think of Peter Powlison, a master teacher, a master's champion in swimming, and a master at creating PrimeTime. In the early '80s, I interviewed Powlison as part of a class in wellness I was teaching. My idea was to interview people who were known for their positive approach to life and in the process to discover their secret for successful living. In Powlison's case, I found a man who was absolutely at peace with himself, totally confident in his ability, and completely sure of his position in life. Powlison was grateful for his life, he lived in a state of readiness, he radiated a sense of calmness.

At one point in our interview, I asked him to describe his mental state prior to having open-heart surgery. Specifically, I asked him if he was afraid of the operation. Our class sat in awe as he described lying on the operating table and being completely relaxed, completely ready for an operation that strikes fear in me as I write about it. Powlison said in response to my question, "I was at peace. At that moment I turned my life over to God. I said, God, my life is in your hands, please let your will be done." At the most critical moment in his life, Powlison was confident; he was ready; he was not afraid; he did not have anxiety. To be confident, ready, calm, and relaxed in the face of your biggest challenge is the essence of being grateful.

Powlison had the confidence and the psychological readiness to know that he could lecture to an auditorium full of people, he could swim in a National Master's Championship, and he could face a life-threatening event. In all areas of performance, Powlison looked forward to giving his best effort; he was relaxed and calm.

**Excited** As you contemplate moments of PrimeTime, you are excited. Excited, in HiLevel terms, is the ability to focus under pressure. Excited is the state of physical and emotional readiness where you can focus during the most important moments of your competition or performance. Your physical and emotional training has given you the ability to focus at this level.

I think of Robby Naish. The following story comes from Darrell Wong. The scene is Ho'okipa. The year is 1989. The event is a slalom race. The format is a flying start from outside the surf to the beach and then back out around the buoy with the finish on the beach. The surf is six to eight feet and as they go around the buoy at the beach and head back out into the surf an eight-foot wave is looming on the horizon. Robby is slightly ahead of the pack as they approach the buoy. The wave in question is about to break outside the buoy.

In an instant, Robby completes a duck jib around the buoy, in front of the wave, underneath the lip, and races to the beach, emerging as the winner. The other competitors choose to play it safe and go over the wave and then around the buoy. Robby decided in the heat of the moment, with the event and his health on the line, to go for it.

The fact that Robby did this maneuver on slalom equipment with the risk of wiping out and going over the falls is evidence of his spontaneity, his courage, his true competitive nature, and his ability to focus. His actions in this instance are a perfect example of what it means to be excited, to focus under pressure. In this pressure-packed situation, he was able to *think* about what he needed to do and translate his thoughts into the *feelings* required (edge control, balance and upper body quickness and strength) to complete his transition underneath the lip of the wave. The excitement he generated in this situation originated in his love of windsurfing, love of competition, and absolute belief in himself and his ability. Naish has exceptional talent and an exceptional ability to generate excitement.

**Committed**    As you contemplate moments of PrimeTime, you are committed. Committed, in HiLevel terms, means that you are willing to accept the responsibility for making it happen. Committed is the state of being eager to make a decision and follow through with the right choices.

## PrimeTime's Destination

The HiLevel process involves hard work to increase your mental toughness (the belief that you can do it); ability to focus (the feeling that you are doing it); and follow-through (the choice that you will do it).

In the introduction of this book, I referred to the HiLevel process as a set of directions for getting from point A to point B. PrimeTime is point B. In the metaphor of life as a journey, PrimeTime is a place you

# Kenny Bradshaw
# =
# Commitment

I think of Kenny Bradshaw. Bradshaw is committed to riding the biggest waves ever ridden. He wants to do tow-ins at a spot called Wailua Rivermouth on a day when Waimea Bay closes out. By conservative estimates we are talking about a wave in the neighborhood of forty feet.

I recently asked Bradshaw about his commitment to surf in these conditions. His response:

> *"I'm obsessed with the idea of commit-ment and what it means to me. I have never walked away from a day saying that the surf was too big. My commitment is to ride the outer reef on the norh shore of Oahu on a truly huge day. I believe in myself and my ability. I know in my core that my commitment is to ride the biggest waves ever ridden. I want, more than anything, to feel what it is like to be there on a day when the surf is this big. I want to experience what it is like to ride a wave that large. I will not back away from this challenge."*

Bradshaw wanted to ride a forty-foot wave and he was totally committed to making it happen. On January 28, 1998, a day that will be remembered in the surfing world as "Big Wednesday," Kenny was towed into a forty-footer and surpassed his dream. From crest to trough, the face of the wave Kenny rode was at least sixty-five feet high.

work hard to get to, a final destination. When you arrive, you will experience some or all of the following:

**Your skills are working.** In the words of Robby Naish, it's "that really good day at Diamond Head when everything clicks."

**You can focus.** Recalling Csikszentmihalyi: "Concentration is so intense that there is no attention left over to think about anything irrelevant, or to worry about problems." Several athletes have reported to me that during moments of PrimeTime they are so focused that a bomb could go off and it would not distract them. Golfer Tony Jacklin describes this level of focus: "When I'm in this state, this cocoon of concentration, I'm living fully in the present, not moving out of it. I'm aware of every half inch of my swing. I'm absolutely engaged, involved in what I'm doing at that particular moment."

Baseball players talk about being able to see the writing on the ball or that the ball comes up to the plate looking like a balloon. Chess players talk about PrimeTime as a time when they can see the total board, when their moves reflect their ability to become one with the game. René Tillich talks about PrimeTime relative to doing therapy: "During moments of PrimeTime, I know exactly what I am doing, I know exactly where I am going with the patient. I know what they are going to think before they think it."

**You are having fun.** By your standards, you are on fire. For some people fun has to do with laughs, satisfaction, winning, getting better, etc. Your experience is dictated by the feelings of joy and love associated with doing well at what you love to do. Joe Willie Namath: "It's pretty hard to describe how that feels, throwing a touchdown pass and seeing the referee throw his arms in the air, signaling a touchdown, signaling that you've done just what you set out to do. It's an incredible feeling. It's like your whole body's bursting with happiness."

Your body bursting with happiness is what weightlifters refer to as the "pump," and what Samuel Fussell, author of the book *Muscle*, refers to as "the glow, the magic pump." Fussell draws the following analogy as he returns to the weight room, wondering if he can recapture this feeling.

*"I'd start slowly, warming up, testing
myself, and then it would happen.
Release. From exercise to exercise I'd go,*

*feeling as if I were driving a car on a dark, wet night in the city. Suddenly, the stoplight just ahead turns green, the next one green, and green again. You don't need to brake for even one light. All you see is the road before you. You're not quite sure why, but you are going the right speed at the right place and time. You take a quick look at the speedometer. Just to memorize the reading. But there's no need. Just keep it going, another light, another block, another weight, another exercise. Green, green, green."*

Fussell gives a poetic rendering to the feeling you know well if you have learned to love training with weights. The feeling that goes with reaching PrimeTime, the feeling that goes with being in the flow of lifting, the feeling that you are, according to Fussell, "going the right speed at the right place and time."

You are, in fact, in an altered state of consciousness. You feel invincible, you feel relaxed, and yet your mind, body, and spirit are working together as one. Your actions reflect your inner harmony. Your mind is clear. Your body is singing and your spirit is alive. I remember making a talk on the essence of PrimeTime and a little lady with white hair was sitting in the front row nodding her head in agreement throughout my talk. After my talk I made a point to find her and ask her why she seemed to be so familiar with my remarks. She smiled and said, "I know exactly what you are talking about, I put myself in that state every day when I needlepoint. My hands take over and whatever I think about, my fingers can do. The colors seem brighter. My sense of time disappears. All of my aches and pains are gone and I am totally relaxed." A lifetime of practice had brought this lady to a place where PrimeTime was a regular part of her life.

You feel in control. You let *it* go, that is, your concern about the outcome, your consideration about how you are doing, your fear about getting hurt or embarrassed, your preoccupation with doing it right. Joe Green, former All-Pro Defensive Tackle, said of being in this state,

> *"It feels beautiful. You are going all out. You are full of the desire to succeed. You are full of power. . . of superior confidence. You reach a peak in every part of your being. You reach an emotional high, a physical high, all of them together. It's almost like being possessed. But while it is kind of a frenzy, of wild action. . . you are never out of control. You have great awareness of everything that is happening around you and your part in the whole."*

PrimeTime is a final destination, a place you get to when you are doing really well at something that is important to you. To experience PrimeTime you will have learned how to: Live in the moment, maintain an awareness of present-time activities. Bring a sense of joy to your activity. Love what you do. Do what you love. Maintain your focus, eliminate distractions. Contemplate the desired outcome, see and feel it. Bring the feeling of success to the event in question.

## PrimeTime's Satisfaction

The satisfaction of creating PrimeTime has to do with your ability to take a few moments and contemplate the meaning of what just happened. While the experience is fresh in your mind and your body is still buzzing, take the time to:

Graciously accept the results of your efforts. See and feel everything that went into the creation of PrimeTime. The feelings related to doing well at what you love to do (remember momentum in Step 4) are a precious source of fuel, and this fuel can be used to create moments of PrimeTime in the future.

Acknowledge yourself and the contribution of others. Give thanks to the source of your power. The ability to acknowledge yourself and others in this way is a huge emotional deposit that builds trust and humility (remember Trust in Step 6).

Internalize and record the learning gained from your efforts. Give thanks again and celebrate. The ability to record this learning will en-

*PrimeTime is a final destination, a place you get to when you are doing really well at something that is important to you. To experience PrimeTime you will have learned how to: Live in the moment, maintain an awareness of present-time activities. Bring a sense of joy to your activity. Love what you do. Do what you love. Maintain your focus, eliminate distractions. Contemplate the desired outcome, see and feel it. Bring the feeling of success to the event in question.*

hance your ability to experience growth (remember growth in Step 7).

Evaluate your performance, anticipate, and implement change as needed. Note that the clarity that comes with the creation of PrimeTime will allow you to continue to take risks and be safe.

Focus on the balance of work, play, rest and relaxation in your life. Note that the feelings related to this balance will allow you to take good care of yourself.

Get back to work: Begin the process again. And note that the creation of PrimeTime can be a reminder that hard work got you there and hard work will allow you to return for more.

## PrimeTime and Team

When a team arrives at PrimeTime you can see and feel the teamwork; you can see and feel the fire. Michael Novak once wrote,

> *"When a collection of individuals first jells as a team, truly begins to react as a five-headed or eleven-headed unit rather that an aggregate of five or eleven individuals, you can almost hear the click: a new kind of reality comes into existence at a new level of human development. A basketball team, for example, can click into and out of this reality many times during the same*

*game; and each player, as well as the coach
and the fans, can detect the difference. . . .
For those who have participated on a team
that has known the click of communality,
the experience is unforgettable, like that of
having attained, for a while at least, a
higher level of existence: existence as it
ought to be."*

The reference to communality is similar to what Senator Bill Bradley calls "meshed." Says Bradley,

*"The sudden rush of awareness that a
group has become a meshed team provides
each member with a remarkable sense of
power. Each game is eagerly anticipated.
Road trips suddenly seem like a paid
vacation. You begin to see in your teammates good qualities that before went
unnoticed. The timing of plays becomes
perfect. When members of a team buy into
the program at this level, you achieve
unity but not at the expense of individual
imagination."*

The "new reality" that Novak refers to and the "power" that Bradley refers to are part of the psychological state that is created when a team is able to follow the HiLevel steps to PrimeTime.

## PrimeTime and Peak Experiences

The intense feelings of joy and love that are associated with PrimeTime can be experienced in other areas of your life. Maslow referred to these moments as peak experiences, moments where you feel: the love in a special relationship; the fellowship at a special event; inspiration de-rived from beauty; and satisfaction from an accomplishment.

The feelings associated with peak experiences are special, and they are a reward for living your life with integrity. You have made decisions that were right for you; you have followed up with the appropriate choices, and the intense feelings of joy and love that you experience from time to time are the payoff. Nice going by *you*!

PrimeTime and peak experiences are different and occur for different reasons. PrimeTime occurs because you have worked hard to reach a destination; peak experiences occur because you have been true to yourself. PrimeTime occurs because you have followed a plan, a specific course of action; peak experiences occur at random, often when you least expect them.

PrimeTime and peak experiences are the same in that they are both HiLevel. PrimeTime involves a commitment to the HiLevel process, to performing a particular skill at a particular level. Peak experiences involve a commitment to HiLevel living, to establish certain priorities in your life based on what is important to you.

## Summary

PrimeTime is defined as those special moments associated with doing the activity you love the most. In terms of your performance, PrimeTime has to with the feelings related to one or more of the following: overcoming a challenge; being in a particular physiological state; the satisfaction of reaching a goal and/or the thrill of winning.

The requirements for experiencing PrimeTime have to do with the need to: feel challenged; make full use of your skills; focus completely and measure your success.

*The eight steps which make up the HiLevel process provide toughness training:* the opportunity to develop your mental toughness to the point where a belief about something you want to accomplish becomes an expectation. Mark Richards relates what it was like to surf against Wayne "Rabbit" Bartholomew: "I think Rabbit found it pretty easy to psyche people out because he was so up and ready all of the time. You went into a heat with Rabbit and you knew he wasn't tentatively thinking 'can I beat this guy?' He just knew he could win." Rabbit had worked so hard to develop his mental toughness that he was convinced he could beat you and win. I remember watching Rabbit surf at Sunset Point and being impressed with his mental toughness, as he took off on the most difficult waves and made it look easy. The blueprint for Rabbit's success was hard work.

*The eight steps which make up the HiLevel process provide sensitivity training:* the opportunity to develop the awareness of your feelings and to focus at the level where you become totally absorbed. Robert Deindorfer says about the art of fly-fishing, "No mere mechanical skill. . . no great combination of rod, reel, line and fly will produce over a period of time unless the particular person manages to develop a soundproof, weatherproof, foolproof attention span." Ade Scott, one of the all time great fly-fisherman, said, "I wouldn't hear a gun if they shot it off alongside me."

*The eight steps provide clarity training:* the opportunity to develop your ability to make clear decisions that result in the creation of PrimeTime. Csikszentmihalyi talks about the power of a decision to give direction to your mind and to your life.

> *"Ironically, most people who work experience a more enjoyable state of mind on the job than at home. At work it is clear what needs to be done, and there is clear information about how well one is doing. Yet few people would willingly work more and have less leisure time. Those who do are pitied as workaholics. Generally unnoticed is the fact that the work we want to avoid is actually more satisfying than the free time we try to get more of."*

# Conclusion

The Steps in Review: You have been snowboarding once and you have decided to go twice a year. You live in Hawaii.

## Step 1: What Do You Want To Achieve?

You know what you want to achieve. You have defined PrimeTime in terms of your performance. You want to be the best that you can be and you have accepted the reality that goes with living in Hawaii: limited time on the slopes.

## Step 2: Create The Time and Energy You Need.

You have a plan and you are eager to create the time and energy to make it happen. You are cross-training with in-line skates and working on building the leg strength that is so important in edge control.

## Step 3: Light Your Own Fire.

You know you can Light Your Own Fire. You are mentally tough. You can focus and you are committed. You can show up on the slopes confident in your ability to learn and get better, physically and emotionally ready to give your best effort, and committed to get the most out of every moment.

## Step 4: Maintain the Momentum.

You can maintain your focus. You are clear about what you love to do. With each run you feel yourself getting better; after each day and/or trip your commitment is strengthened.

# Fuel the Fire

## HiLevel Performance
# PRIMETIME

**GROWTH**

**TRUST**

**AWARENESS**  **COMMITMENT**

**MOMENTUM**

**CONFIDENCE**  **FITNESS**  **ACCEPTANCE**

**DESIRE**

**ENERGY**

## Step 5: Refine the Focus.

You have refined your focus. You are aware of how good you can be. Your commitment is set.

## Step 6: Build Trust.

You have learned to build trust, in yourself and in your performance. You have complete confidence in your ability within your accepted range of difficulty.

## Step 7. Experience Growth.

You have learned to experience growth, to put your best effort on the line and accept the results. You are eager to take risks, to push your limits, or to play it safe and stay within your limits. You are comfortable with your ability and you experience PrimeTime.

## Step 8. Create PrimeTime.

You have learned to create PrimeTime, to maintain the state of being grateful, excited, and committed. You experience one or more of the feelings that are important to you relative to: overcoming a challenge, being in a particular physiological state, reaching a goal and/or being the best or winning. Each time you snowboard you feel challenged, make full use of your skills, focus completely, and have a way of measuring your success.

## Congratulations!

## You're There!

# Appendix

# Forced
# DownTime

*"Between stimulus and response,
man has the freedom to choose."*

—Victor Frankl

You experience forced downtime when you are out of action due to an illness or injury. Your challenge is to manage this time well in order to refine your focus, increase clarity, and restore your strength and faith. In the process you may also discover a lesson that your illness or injury represents to you. Be sure to return to action only when you are ready and able to perform at your best, completely well from illness, or healed from injury.

If you have experienced forced downtime, you know firsthand its emotional and physical pain. While you are not always in control of the severity of downtime—as Frankl points out—at least you always have the freedom to choose how you will respond to it. In your response, be proactive.

**1)** **Complete an Evaluation:** Successfully confront the reality of your situation.

**2)** **Develop a Strategy:** Select the proper treatment, process negative thoughts and feelings, and reframe your attitude.

**3)** **Execute a Plan:** Follow a consistent course of action.

# Complete an Evaluation

When you are confronted with forced downtime, an accurate evaluation of your situation can be painful. It will demand that you be open. You may have to hear that you will be out of the action for awhile or that your options for treatment involve serious rehabilitation. Given the sensitivity of this feedback, you may need emotional support in listening to and dealing with this information.

Talk to friends, coaches, trainers, and people with similar situations and backgrounds. People close to you can give you support and feedback regarding your fear, anger, or failure to confront the situation. Seek professional feedback, get a first, second, third and/or fourth opinion. Listen to different views about your situation. This can provide you with the awareness you need to select the proper treatment.

Failure to confront the reality head-on may indicate that you are employing a defense mechanism. Is your mind protecting you from the uncomfortable reality? Resistance may take one or more of these forms:

**Simple Avoidance:** You have the awareness that you need to deal with your situation, but you don't take action; for example, you forget to tell the trainer you are hurt.

**Repression:** You "stuff it away" or attempt to prevent the situation from surfacing in full awareness. You continue to perform, but with only occasional flashes of insight regarding your illness or injury.

**Projection:** Here you are angry about your situation and you attribute your anger to the actions of someone or something.

**Displacement:** You are angry and you take your anger out on someone or something, for example, you kick the dog.

**Reaction Formation:** You give "attitude," your actions don't reflect your true feelings, that is, you act like you don't care.

**Regression:** You revert back to childlike behavior such as pouting or throwing a tantrum.

**Rationalization:** A cousin of avoidance, you overtly begin to make excuses and justify your actions. You make statements such as, "No one's perfect!"

**Outright Denial:** You fail to recognize that you have a situation. You continue to work out when you are sick or injured and in obvious pain and discomfort.

**Attachment:** You are stuck. You are bound to a decision or a feeling that prevents you from responding to your situation. You may say to yourself, "I do not get sick!" or "I can work out whenever I want!"

Consider this scenario: You are injured and are experiencing the frustration and anger associated with forced downtime. In your mind, you know you need to rest and wait until your injury heals before you get back into the action, yet you feel the need to be active today.

Your friends have called and they want you to join them for a strenuous hike. Again, in your mind, you know you need to say no, yet a huge part of you wants to say, "Yes, I'm up for it!" You feel torn, you feel pulled, you practice saying "No" and you feel horrible. You practice saying "Yes" and you feel guilty.

What's going on here? The basis for your decision is a really simple one: you are injured and you need to rest. Why can't you see the simple truth of your situation? Because you are attached to a belief that you are different, tougher and/or stronger than someone who gets hurt and has to say "No" to an invitation to get physical. In truth, the image you have of yourself, your identity, prevents you from seeing the reality of the situation.

In the short-term, defense mechanisms will protect you from seeing the truth and experiencing its associated emotions. In the long-term, defense mechanisms can prevent you from taking good care of yourself. Awareness of these mechanisms is essential.

In truth, your self worth is not tied to your ability to get and be physical. When you permit yourself to experience the emotional pain of forced downtime, you tap the maturity needed to help you shed outdated or counter-productive feelings and decisions.

## Suggested activities:
– Search the literature. Seek to understand the nature of your downtime situation and recommended treatments. You may find the internet helpful in this regard.
– Spend quality time alone in serious contemplation or prayer. Review step two, which calls for spiritual renewal.

## Develop a Strategy
The risk of illness and injury is part of the price you pay for being physically active. The greater the demands you place on your body, the greater the risk to your well-being. In the event that you do get sick or experience an injury, you need to develop a strategy that will help you select the proper treatment, process negative thoughts and feelings, and reframe your attitude.

As preventative medicine is the best medicine, the human body-to-machine analogy works well. My dear friend Ed Nieto used to say, "Fix the machine before it breaks." A back-hoe driver, Ed referred to himself as a "dirt tramp" and his livelihood depended on his ability to operate his machine. Forced downtime for Nieto meant he didn't get paid. If you depend on your body to be able to perform, fix it before it breaks; that is, listen closely to the messages it sends you: rest when you need to, respond quickly to red flags indicating possible injury, ice your sore muscles.

## Selecting the proper treatment

Start by examining your mental toughness and ability to focus, then reinforce your commitment. There is a thin line between the mental toughness that allows you to play through pain, and the mental toughness that allows you to rest or take a day off to recover. Be smart. Physically and emotionally, you need to be aware of your body's needs. Spiritually, the decision you make relative to possible solutions needs to feel right. Listen closely to the messages your body sends you and respond accordingly. The bottom line is that you need to get better in order to give your best effort.

Illnesses and injuries can be broken down into the following categories:

1) **Minor illnesses and injuries:** colds, allergies, cuts, bruises, and slight strains and sprains. Note that the key in terms of slight strains and sprains is no loss in range of motion or function. Regarding minor illnesses and injuries, you have a wide range of options: namely, rest versus continued participation or limited activity, prescription drugs versus natural remedies, ice or heat packs, and a combination of these options.

2) **Serious illnesses and injuries:** flu-like symptoms, broken bones, pulled muscles, and torn ligaments, etc. The defining factor for a serious illness is the presence of a fever. Note that exercising with a fever is dangerous: you run the risk of dehydration and possible damage to internal organs such as the heart, liver, kidneys, and brain. The defining factors for serious injuries are the presence of pain, swelling, loss of range of motion and function, and the risk of making the injury worse. Regarding serious illnesses and injuries, your options are limited and you need medical assistance.

**3)** **Serious injury and you may need an operation:** the injury does not pose an immediate threat to your well-being (elective surgery). In this case, you need to be extremely careful in selecting proper treatment. Consider those athletes who have had operations and gone through rehab and come back to perform at their best. Consider also athletes who have gone through operations and have not been able to return to the action. Having been through three successful surgeries—nose, elbow, and neck—I can speak to the issue of selecting the right treatment. In each case, I sought numerous opinions and was amazed at the range of treatments outlined for each operation. For me, choosing the right treatment came down to feeling comfortable with the doctor, and sensing that the doctor knew and cared about me. Should you be faced with the need to choose the proper treatment for an injury that involves an operation, the decision you make will need to be made in this manner. I probably need not say that much has been written about the importance of the relationship between doctor and patient and the resulting success of the operation and/or treatment.

**4)** **Serious injury and you definitely need an operation:** the injury does pose an immediate threat to your well-being and you do not have the luxury of selecting the proper treatment. In this case, you have no choice but to make the best of your situation. At this point you must draw on the strength of your faith and do everything in your power to prepare yourself for the operation.

## Process negative thoughts and feelings

Your negative feelings about your situation need to be recognized and processed. Their recognition is both natural and healthy. Make the time to accept your feelings and talk about them with people who support you, and then let them go. The negative feelings serve you to the degree you learn from them and recognize their presence as evidence of how much you care. Emotions of anger, grief, failure, resentment, and regret are known to suppress the immune system directly by nerves and neurochemicals and indirectly through the secretion of stress-related hormones in the blood. These negative emotions, while easy to understand, can work against the healing process.

It is important to note, regarding physical pain and discomfort, that your pain. The Lamaze and Bradley methods were described in Step. 6, to build trust in the relationship between your pain and your attitude. A study at Johns Hopkins "suggests that 'positive thinking' may help you cope with pain better, while negative thoughts may worsen the pain by intensifying the anxiety you have about hurting."

## Reframe your attitude

The ability to reframe your attitude will allow you to choose those thoughts and feelings that will support you in maintaining a good attitude. The reframe process was covered in detail in Step 5, Refine the Focus.

Begin by defining your condition. Again, remember to reserve judgment and be patient with yourself. Ask yourself these questions:

**1)**   What are the positive aspects of this issue?

**2)**   What is the upset related to this issue?

**3)**   What am I eager to do to resolve this issue?

**4)**   What will be my focus in resolving this issue?

**5)**   How can I take pride in my ability to reframe this issue?

The athletes who do the best job in reframing forced downtime are the ones who follow a relaxed pattern of handling desires to get better, that is, they "deal" without creating internal conflict for themselves. They allow the solutions to surface naturally, trusting their own abilities to manage and effectively utilize the healing properties of mind and body. As Claude Bouchard, et al, point out clearly in their book *Exercise, Fitness and Health:* deprivation of exercise can lead to irritability, anxiety, and depression. These feelings are normal and can be thought of as a natural part of the healing process.

Acceptance, as it relates to a serious injury, is similar to *acceptance* as the term is used by Elizabeth Kubler-Ross in her book *On Death and Dying*. Her four psychological stages of acceptance are: denial, anger, depression, and acceptance.

In denial, you refuse to acknowledge the injury. To prolong this phase you seek endless opinions, while your body is busy sending you signals that you are hurt.

In anger, you blame yourself or somebody. To prolong this phase you take out your anger on yourself, train in obvious discomfort, and give yourself "attitude."

In depression, your anger has turned inward and your thinking is distorted and extremely negative. To prolong this phase, you are impatient and you refuse to see the big picture or review your situation in an objective manner.

In acceptance, you develop a realistic plan of rehab and you begin to dedicate yourself to what is required. The ability to accept your situation will require the same mental toughness, focus, and follow-through needed to give your best effort in the heat of your athletic performance.

Your best effort during forced downtime involves maintaining a positive attitude, being patient and good to yourself, setting realistic goals for your recovery, and working hard to achieve them. As an athlete you are used to working hard in practice and seeing the results of your efforts in your performance. In forced downtime, the emphasis is on rest and rehabilitation and the results of your efforts may be harder and more frustrating to evaluate. The acceptance of your situation involves the coordination of mental, physical, and spiritual energy to focus on completing recovery and returning to the action. You will need to relax and generate positive attitudes and beliefs.

## Suggested activities:

While listening to the music of your choice, focus on your breathing, deep muscle relaxation, and feelings of well-being. Repeat this exercise twice a day for twenty minutes a session. Laugh, enjoy good food, read, and spend quality time with your family. The latest mental training advice for people who are sick, injured or recovering from surgery was covered in depth in Step 4, Maintain the Momentum.

There are three mental training skills that relate specifically to rehabilitation.

**1)** **Feeling Good** Scenes are imagined that produce positive feelings such as enthusiasm, pride and confidence related to a successful rehab. I suggest adding music to this exercise.

**2)** **Back to the Action** Scenes are imagined that take you from where you are now to the successful completion of your rehab and a return to the action of your activity. See yourself performing at your very best.

**3)** **Solutions** Scenes are imagined that produce solutions to the challenges of your rehab, i.e., returning to the action of your activity wearing a knee brace.

Practice these skills in a way that makes sense given your situation. Physically and emotionally, you will need to find activities that stimulate your interest and excitement and allow you to be as physically and emotionally involved as possible. The feelings associated with rehab may be new and somewhat sedate compared to the excitement of training and performing up to your standards.

## Suggested activities:

*On a physical level,* work with a trainer or physical therapist to find the proper exercises. In general, walk, stretch and do whatever you can to elevate your heart rate and maintain your cardiovascular conditioning. In the case of ankle or knee injuries, complete rehabilitation is associated with the balance of strength of the bones, tendons, ligaments, intrinsic and proprioceptor muscles that support the joint. A word of caution: There is an adjustment phase when this critical balance is established. Be careful not to rush back into the action as you will risk further injury. A simple criterion for ankle or knee injuries is your ability to hop in a normal pattern on your injured leg. For all injuries, you should be pain-free for about seven days before returning to full activity or competition.

*On an emotional level,* practice feeling the excitement related to your recovery. The key here is to focus on already having the physical recovery you want to have. Practice "thinking in a feeling sense," "see" your recovery in living color and "feel" it with passion. Spiritually, you need to be motivated to complete your rehab and return to the action.

## Suggested activities:

Affirm the commitment you have made to do the work on a daily basis. Share your progress with people who support you and your commitment. Surround yourself with positive reminders that you have what it takes to get the job done. You must be willing to do the work needed to recover from your situation. In the case of illness and some injuries, the most important work is rest. In the case of injuries, the work involved is rehabilitation exercise. In the case of physical disability, the work is in learning to adapt. Are you willing to do the work needed to return to your activity? Your answer needs to be part of the commitment you have made to yourself and your recovery. During the course of your forced downtime, your commitment will be tested in keeping with the severity of your situation. There will be times when you will need to push yourself, to work hard, even when you want to quit. In order to move through your negative thoughts and feelings, you will want to reframe your resistance into movement and your fear into excitement. You will need to continue to believe in yourself and your ability to do the work, feel the excitement and make the right choices.

## Execute a Plan

In forced downtime, a plan will allow you to record your intention and attention for recovery. Intention is what you want to achieve. Attention is the management of time and energy in a way that supports optimal recovery. You must be aggressively active at every step in your rehab.

## Suggested activities:

**1)** Set up a calendar to record important dates regarding doctors appointments, rehabilitation sessions and related activities.

**2)** Include a section for recording pulse, vital statistics, and general physical progress.

**3)** Include a journal to record thoughts, feelings and insights regarding your experience. Write about and process your negative feelings according to a timetable.

**4)** Watch your diet and weigh yourself regularly. Claude Bouchard, et al, point out in their book that periods of inactivity can result in excess levels of insulin, which means that excess calories will be stored as fat. During periods of forced downtime you might consider reducing your caloric intake.

## Summary

Forced downtime is an intense time filled with emotions and opportunities for personal awareness and growth. As you evaluate your situation, you have the ability to choose your response. The ability to accept your situation, to coordinate your mental, physical and spiritual energy to focus on recovery, will be a test. The mental toughness, focus, and follow-through needed to complete your plan for recovery and return to your activity will make you a stronger person. Forced downtime is a time for reflection, an opportunity to redefine commitment to your health, fitness, performance, and personal growth.

I especially admire the way Itula Mili of Brigham Young University handled his situation. A tight end playing in his last college game, Mili caught a pass and as he turned to run up field he was tackled from the side. His body turned but his leg stayed in place. The damage to his knee was gruesome: anterior collateral, medial collateral, and posterior collateral ligaments were shredded.

Projected as a first-round draft choice, Mili's career was thought to be over. After three hours of reconstructive surgery and six months of rehab he is now projected to play in the National Football League. Throughout his rehab, Mili accepted the support of his teammates and his family and drew on the strength of his Mormon faith.

Today he says,

> *"I'm optimistic about things. Things will work out; I just have to keep working harder and there is still a lot of work to be done. I think the injury helped me to put things in perspective. Injuries occur to everyone. No one knows when it's going to happen to them. When it does and it ends a career, you have to remember there's life after football and it's a long life."*

He adds that he has used the skepticism that some have expressed about his ability to play again as a source of motivation. "For me I take that skepticism as a driving force and a driving motivation. . . to prove to people that I can make it through this thing."

Mili met the challenge of forced downtime head-on and for now it seems he has won. As he completes his rehab, he continues to refine focus, learn from the situation and generate the fire necessary to play professional football.

Consider the following points about managing forced downtime.

**Pain:** Various mental training skills are specifically designed to help manage physical and emotional pain.

**Honesty:** The ability to evaluate your situation and choose your own response reflects the trust you have in yourself.

**Clarity:** The ability to generate positive beliefs and attitudes about your situation will aid recovery.

**Strength:** The ability to light your own fire and focus on complete recovery are evidence of character.

**Growth:** The ability to complete your recovery and return to the action will give you a new appreciation of your mind, body and spirit.

As a final example, I would like to mention the experience of Carrie Hironaka, who has endured and gained from the pain and frustration of forced downtime. In her junior year in high school, she played varsity volleyball, softball and basketball, a first team All-Star in softball and basketball. At the end of her basketball season, she was selected to play in an All-Star game. At a routine practice, she went up for a rebound and tore her left ACL (anterior cruciate ligament).

Reconstructive surgery followed and that summer she began what was to be seven months of arduous and painful rehab. She sat out all of her volleyball season and all but two games of her softball season, then she returned to the action. Carrie reported to basketball on time. She was tentative at first, but she quickly returned to full speed and was playing well when she tore her right ACL. Once again, reconstructive surgery followed and she began the process of rehab. Carrie was cleared to play basketball in October of her freshman year in college. She made the team and was playing well when she tore the meniscus cartilage in her left knee. Orthoscopic surgery followed and Carrie went back into rehab for the last two and a half weeks of the season. She reported for softball and played the entire season injury-free. This year as she reports for her sophomore year in college, she plans to play basketball and softball.

When I asked Carrie why, after three operations and countless hours of rehab, she continues to play, her answer was simple: "I cannot imagine my life without the competition of sports and I want to be the one who determines that my athletic career is over. I will never allow an injury to end my career."

When I asked Carrie about the pain of her rehab, she paused and then commented,

> *"The pain associated with regaining the last ten degrees of flexion and extension in both knees was excruciating. However, by far the hardest part of my rehab was getting clearance to play. I had completed the rehab and my Doctor wouldn't let me play. That was the most frustrating thing I have ever been through. I had done all of the work, but I still wasn't allowed to play. I live for the satisfaction that comes with giving everything I have to the spirit of the*

*competition. Sports are an integral part of my life and I plan to compete until I no longer feel this way. The pain and frustration of my injuries has taught me a major lesson in humility. I treasure my health and my ability to compete. My injuries have taught me to appreciate everything I have, to focus in the present and to put everything I have on the line and accept the results. . . including the pain and frustration of injuries."*

# References

## The Fire

*Flow, The Psychology of Optimal Experience* by Mihaly Csikszentmihalyi. HarperCollins Publishers: New York, 1990.

*Mental Training for Peak Performance* by Steven Ungerleider. Rodale Press: Emmaus, Pennsylvania, 1996.

*Psyched to Win, How to master mental skills to improve your physical performance* by Robert M. Nideffer, Ph.D. Leisure Press: Champaign, Illinois, 1992.

*The Seven Spiritual Laws of Success, A Practical Guide to the Fulfillment of Your Dreams* by Deepak Chopra. Amber-Allen Publishing: San Rafael, California, 1994.

*The 7 Habits of Highly Effective People, Powerful Lessons in Personal Change* by Steven Covey. Simon & Schuster: New York, 1989.

**"What's Gotten into Andre Agassi?"** by Ross Wetzsteon. *Men's Journal*, August 1995, Vol. 4, No. 6.

## Step One

*Flow, The Psychology of Optimal Experience* by Mihaly Csikszentmihalyi. HarperCollins Publishers: New York, 1990.

*Hymns to an Unknown God, Awakening the Spirit in Everyday Life* by Sam Keen. Bantam Books: New York, 1994.

## Step Two

*The Book of Quotes* by Barbara Rowes. Ballantine Books: New York, 1979.

*The 7 Habits of Highly Effective People, Powerful Lessons in Personal Change* by Steven Covey. Simon & Schuster: New York, 1989.

## Step Three

**ACHIEVE MORE WITH BETTER BRAIN CHEMISTRY**, Video Tape by Forest S. Tennant, Jr., M.D., Ph.D. Veract, Inc., 1987.

*Performing Your Best: A Guide to Psychological Skills for High Achievers* by Tom Kubistant. Life Enhancement Publications: Champaign, Illinois, 1986.

*Psycho Cybernetics* by Maxwell Maltz, M.D. Melvin Powers Book Company: Hollywood, California, 1960.

## Step Four

*Emotional Intelligence, Why it can matter more than IQ* by Daniel Goleman. Bantam Books: New York, 1995.

"The Hoarse Whisper, Eastwood IN ONE TAKE" by Drew Drury. *Men's Journal*, April 1997, Vol. 6, No. 3.

## Step Five

"AMBY, HIGH SCHOOL RUNNER" by Marc Bloom and Burfoot. *Track & Field*, Spring 1997, Vol. 6, No. 1.

*Sacred Hoops, Spiritual Lessons of a Hardwood Warrior* by Phil Jackson and Hugh Delehanty. Hyperion: New York, 1995.

*The Evolving Self, A Psychology for the Third Millennium* by Mihaly Csikszentmihalyi. HarperCollins Publishers: New York, 1993.

*The Path to Love, Renewing the Power of Spirit in Your Life* by Deepak Chopra. Harmony Books: New York, 1997.

*The 7 Habits of Highly Effective People, Powerful Lessons in Personal Change* by Steven Covey. Simon & Schuster: New York, 1989.

## Step Six

ACHIEVE MORE WITH BETTER BRAIN CHEMISTRY, Video Tape by Forest S. Tennant, Jr., M.D., Ph.D. Veract, Inc., 1987.

*Beyond Success, The 15 Secrets of a Winning Life* by Brian D. Biro. Pygmalion Press: Hamilton, Montana, 1995.

*Flow, The Psychology of Optimal Experience* by Mihaly Csikszentmihalyi. HarperCollins Publishers: New York, 1990.

*Free Yourself from Pain* by Dr. David E. Bressler and Richard Turbo. Simon & Schuster: New York, 1979.

*Love Medicine & Miracles* by Bernie Seigel, M.D. Harper & Row: New York, 1986.

"Over the Edge, Special Report: AWARE THAT DRUG TESTING IS A SHAM, ATHLETES SEEM TO RELY MORE THAN EVER ON BANNED PERFORMANCE ENHANCERS" by Michael Bamberger and Don Yaeger. *Sports Illustrated*, April 14, 1997, Vol. 86, No. 15.

"Punahou Pipeline, Honolulu school is a factory for volleyball legends" by Mia Lambert. *HEAT*, January, 1997, Vol. 1, No. 3.

*Sacred Hoops, Spiritual Lessons of a Hardwood Warrior* by Phil Jackson and Hugh Delehanty. Hyperion: New York, 1995.

*Somatics, Reawakening the Mind's Control of Movement, Flexibility, and Health* by Thomas Hanna. Addison-Wesley Publishing Company: New York, 1988.

*Toward a Psychology of Being* by Abraham H. Maslow. D. Van Nostrand Company: New York, 1962.

# Step Seven

*Creating Affluence, Wealth Consciousness in the Field of All Possibilities* by Deepak Chopra. Amber-Allen Publishing: New York, 1993.

**Elliot Eisner, Pan Pacific Conference,** Video Tape, Punahou School, 1996.

*Grist for the Mill* by Ram Dass and Stephen Levine. Unity Press: Santa Cruz, California, 1976.

*Most of All They Taught Me Happiness, Years of war, moments of peace, and lessons in living from extraordinary people* by Robert Muller. Image Books: New York, 1985.

*Psyched to Win, How to master mental skills to improve your physical performance* by Robert M. Nideffer, Ph.D. Leisure Press: Champaign, Illinois, 1992.

*Psycho Cybernetics, A New Way to Get More out of Life* by Maxwell Maltz, M.D. Melvin Powers Book Company: Hollywood, California, 1960.

*Sacred Hoops, Spiritual Lessons of a Hardwood Warrior* by Phil Jackson and Hugh Delehanty. Hyperion: New York, 1995.

*Spontaneous Healing* by Andrew Weil, M.D. Alfred A. Knopf: New York, 1995.

*The Path to Love, Renewing the Power of Spirit in Your Life* by Deepak Chopra. Harmony Books: New York, 1997.

"**Windsurfing for a Better Zen**" by Annabella Hofman. *American Windsurfer*, January, 1997, Vol. 1, No. 3.

*You'll See It When You Believe It!* by Dr. Wayne N. Dyer. William Morrow and Company: New York, 1989.

# Step Eight

*Ageless Body, Timeless Mind, The Quantum Alternative to Growing Old* by Deepak Chopra. Harmony Books: New York, 1993.

*Flow, The Psychology of Optimal Experience* by Mihaly Csikszentmihalyi. HarperCollins Publishers: New York, 1990.

*Mark Richards, A Surfing Legend* by David Knox. Angus & Robertson: Pymble NSW, Australia, 1992.

*Muscle* by Samuel Wilson Fussell. Avon Books: New York, 1991.

*Transcendent Experiences in Sports* by Michael Murphy and Rhea White. Penguin Books: New York, 1995.

"**You Can't Buy Heart**" by Bill Bradley. *Sports Illustrated*, October 31, 1977, Vol. 47, No. 18.

# Appendix

*Exercise, Fitness and Health. A Consensus of Current Knowledge* by Claude Bouchard, et al. Human Kinetics Books: Illinois, 1998.

*Flow, The Psychology of Optimal Experience* by Mihaly Csikszentmihalyi. HarperCollins Publishers: New York, 1990.

"**Mili's confident he will come back**" by Curtis Murayama. *Honolulu Advertiser*, April 18, 1997.

# Acknowledgments

As a writer, I have learned to express my fire and to be patient. Thanks to Harry Grzelewski and several other key people, I know how to express my interest, intensity, excitement and passion for sports psychology. I have also learned patience. To get the words "book" and "finished" in the same sentence requires hard work and patience.

I have been blessed at Punahou School. I have received just the right blend of support and challenge to create a class and write a book that gives my life both direction and meaning. At the end of this year, I will have taught here for thirty years. As I prepare to move on to the next step, I am grateful to all of you who have allowed me to do my work and to be part of your life.

I have received tremendous support from many inspirational athletes, coaches, friends, teachers, administrators, and other parents. While the story of how I came to write *Fuel the Fire* is complex, and involved many deeply meaningful lessons, I could not have completed this book without the support and love of my family. I thank you Elise, Reyn, Shannon. . . .